COMMON GROUND
ON TERRORISM

COMMON GROUND ON TERRORISM

Soviet-American Cooperation
Against the Politics of Terror

Edited by

IGOR BELIAEV

and

JOHN MARKS

W·W·NORTON & COMPANY

New York London

The text of this book is composed in Plantin.
Composition and manufacturing by the Haddon Craftsmen, Inc.
Book design by Jacques Chazaud.

First Edition.

Library of Congress Cataloging-in-Publication Data
Common ground on terrorism : Soviet-American cooperation against the
    politics of terror / edited by Igor Beliaev and John Marks.
        p.   cm.
    1. Terrorism—Prevention—International cooperation.
    2. Terrorism—United States. 3. Terrorism—Soviet Union. 4. Soviet
    Union—Foreign relations—United States. 5. Soviet Union—Foreign
    relations—United States.   I. Beliaev, I. P. (Igor' Petrovich)
    II. Marks, John D.
    HV6431.C6473 1991
    363.3'2'0947—dc20   90–21173

ISBN 0–393–02986–7

W.W. Norton & Company, Inc., 500 Fifth Avenue, New York, N.Y. 10110
W.W. Norton & Company, Ltd., 10 Coptic Street, London WC1A 1PU

1 2 3 4 5 6 7 8 9 0

Contents

6

Acknowledgments

In the Soviet Union, often the most difficult element in launching a new project is securing permission. In the United States, there exists permission to do virtually anything; the problem is usually finding enough funds to pay the bill. When setting up the U.S.-Soviet Task Force to Prevent Terrorism, on whose work this book is based, we pooled our collective transcultural skills in obtaining both permission and funding. We are extremely grateful for all those who helped—particularly those who overcame initial skepticism that such a project was possible.

On the American side, we were generously supported by foundations. The first foundation official to recognize the merit of the project and the one without whom the project would probably have died in its infancy is Wade Greene of Rockefeller Family Associates. Wade identified anonymous donors; for their support, which has lasted these last three years, we are extremely grateful.

Former Deputy Secretary of State John Whitehead, time

after time, intervened in our behalf in the foundation world. He has become, in many ways, the American patron of the project, and we are extremely appreciative for his help. John Lockwood and Rufus Jones of ICE-International Cultural Exchange introduced us to Mr. Whitehead and have otherwise provided much needed assistance. The Lippincott Foundation—and particularly Don and Alfred Lippincott—also supplied crucial support. The Lippincotts have stood behind Search for Common Ground from the beginning years, and we could not be more appreciative.

Brian Jenkins of The RAND Corporation not only played a key role on the Task Force, but he put himself at professional risk with his early support. He traveled to Moscow to help set the original agenda, and he later convinced his colleagues at RAND to take on the project. The RAND Corporation, working through Brian, Jim Thompson, and Bruce Hoffman, became a key player in the project, and we were all extremely grateful for RAND's willingness to host, co-sponsor, and provide substantial resources for the Santa Monica meetings. The image of the Soviet participants—and particularly the two retired KGB generals—wandering the halls of the (non-classified) part of RAND will long remained etched in our post-Cold War memory books.

The Carnegie Corporation of New York provided crucial last-minute support for the Santa Monica meetings. Carnegie's Fritz Mosher and Deana Arsenian were extremely helpful in suggesting ways to improve the project.

The Soros Foundation of New York was generous in approving a grant that helped the American side return the gracious welcome the Soviets had furnished in Moscow. The School of Advanced International Studies of Johns Hopkins University awarded the project a stipend and promoted it widely in a monograph and book edited by Simon Serfaty, *The Future of U.S.-Soviet Relations: Twenty American Initiatives for a New Agenda.*

Another anonymous donor was a major financial contributor; to this person, who has been so generous and who has served this project and Search for Common Ground so well, we are extraordinarily grateful. Indeed, many supporters of Search for Common Ground made special contributions to the project. For this and their backing in other projects, we thank them.

Allen Grossman, Board President of Search for Common Ground, played a major part in planning the project in the United States and by traveling to Moscow. He started out with little background on the terrorism issue and wound up making an important substantive contribution. Bonnie Pearlman of Search for Common Ground coordinated the project on the U.S. side, and she could not have done a better job. Her professional competence coupled with her wonderful personal qualities made the Task function in an efficient, humane way. Marguerite Millhauser, also a Task Force member, worked in tandem with Bonnie in planning and designing the meetings. Her process and facilitation skills were critical to enabling the Task Force to achieve more than its founders ever thought possible.

Betsy Cohen of Search for Common Ground arrived late and became a key player. Her Russian language skills and her extensive knowledge of things Soviet greatly enhanced the quality of the project. Rebecca Fox did a fine job in coordinating the project in its early months. Anne Paddock cheerfully retyped chapter after chapter.

Eric Grove, the one member of the U.S.-Soviet Task Force who is neither American nor Soviet, did wonders for this book's readability by editing most of the chapters. Eric struggled to find common ground between Soviet and American authors, and his contribution was enormous. It was also Eric who singlehandedly took on the mission of opening up the Task Force to Western European participation and holding a conference in Moscow. Working through his organization, the Foundation for International Security, he accomplished what most of his colleagues doubted he could ever do. We acknowledge his successes.

On the Soviet side, the Editorial Board of the prestigious Soviet magazine *Literaturnaya Gazeta* (*Literary Gazette*) immediately understood the importance of the fight against international terrorism and provided substantial support for the Task Force from its first days. The magazine generously made available a broad number of personnel and facilities. The American side felt the project truly worked thanks to the efforts of *Literaturnaya Gazeta.*

The Soviet Peace Committee made a significant contribution to the project. It was the Peace Committee that made the American side feel graciously welcome in Moscow, and that supplied excellent facilities, substantial resources, and skilled personnel.

We are extremely grateful to the Committee of State Security of the USSR (KGB) for the participation of retired KGB Lieutenant General Feodor Sherbak and retired Major General Valentin Zvezdenkov. We thank our interpreters who did wonders in cross-cultural communications. They were, on the Soviet side, Professor Alexandr Shveitser and Alexandr Tronfue, and on the American side, Natalie Latter and Dwight Roesch.

We thank the Center for Soviet-American Dialogue and its leader Rama Vernon for organizing the first Soviet-American Citizens' Summit where we met in 1988 and decided to organize the project. What we have since accomplished is totally in keeping with the reason the Summit was held in the first place. We are also grateful for having received an achievement award at the Second Citizens' Summit in Moscow in January 1990.

Lastly, we thank all the Soviet and Western members of the Task Force who are named elsewhere in this book. Their commitment of time, energy, and hard work was at the heart of the Task Force's work and provides the essence of the book.

Igor BELIAEV   John MARKS
for *Literaturnaya Gazeta*   for Search for Common Ground
Moscow   Washington, D.C.

August 1990

COMMON GROUND
ON TERRORISM

CHAPTER 1

Introduction

IGOR BELIAEV AND JOHN MARKS

F or Soviets and Americans alike, terrorism is a particularly
unfortunate fact of modern life. Terrorism threatens the
very fabric of civilization. Unfortunately, even the most effective countermeasures fail to eliminate it. From the point of
view of the terrorists—however misguided—the potential
gains outweigh the risks and costs. To terrorists—whether individuals, groups, or nations—terrorism offers a way to impose their will and gain access to the news media in a world
where real and imagined grievances are not easily heard or
satisfied.

Today, the U.S. and Soviet approaches toward terrorism
are, more and more, coinciding. Important voices in both

Igor Beliaev is a Political Observer (columnist) at the weekly newspaper
Literaturnaya Gazeta in Moscow. John Marks is the Executive Director,
Search for Common Ground; a former Foreign Service Officer; co-author of
The CIA and the Cult of Intelligence; and author of *The Search for the "Man-
churian Candidate."*

Beliaev and Marks are the co-chairs of the Soviet-American Task Force
to Prevent Terrorism, which is sponsored by their two organizations.

countries are urging their governments to work together—to turn the fight against terrorism into a joint struggle. Such an effort would represent for the Soviet Union and the United States a worthy undertaking that makes hardheaded political sense—*if* the two countries are really serious about building a cooperative relationship.

To date, both governments have taken the first steps toward cooperation against terrorism. They have made clear that terrorism is not an acceptable means to achieve any end, and they have stopped accusing each other of supporting international terrorism. While disagreements remain, we believe—and it is the thesis of this book—that the best interests of our two nations will be served by a high level of cooperation in the fight against terrorism.

In our view, increased U.S.-Soviet action against terrorism would produce benefits on three different levels:

1. *Preventing specific acts of terrorism.* Through collaboration, the superpowers would, on occasion, be able to stop actual terrorist attacks. This book will describe a whole array of methods and strategies to make this possible.

2. *Shifting the global climate in which terrorists operate.* Joint Soviet-American action, even on a limited scale, would send a signal to the rest of the world that, despite their remaining differences, the United States and USSR are united in opposing terrorism. The fact that the two countries are cooperating would probably have as much impact as the specifics of the cooperation. Although superpower collaboration obviously would not end the problem of terrorism, it could well reduce the legitimacy of terrorist violence. Both countries would be saying, in effect, that political ends cannot be achieved through terrorist tactics and that perpetrators will be treated as criminals. In recent years as regional conflicts have been winding down, a noticeable—but by no means overwhelming—trend toward the "delegitimization"

of terrorism has emerged. By increased collaboration, the superpowers would be reinforcing this trend.

3. *Strengthening the U.S.-Soviet relationship.* Joint Soviet-American efforts to prevent terrorism would contribute to improving U.S.-Soviet relations, given other favorable conditions. Successful collaboration would be an important confidence-building measure, which would demonstrate that U.S.-Soviet cooperation is possible, even in extremely sensitive areas.

We make our case at a time when the Cold War is coming to an end, and when the United States and USSR have succeeded in draining most of the poison from the relationship. Leaders in both countries are faced with a dramatically changed world, and they are developing new ways to deal with issues that once aggravated the East-West struggle. While the post-World War II security system is disappearing and the replacement system is still in flux, neither country—sensibly—is letting down its guard or disarming unilaterally.

But where the emphasis in the superpower relationship once was on facing the other as the enemy, the emphasis has now shifted toward standing together facing the common danger. Terrorism is a critical part of that common danger. We believe that both our nations should deal with terrorism within a framework similar to that established by Presidents Gorbachev and Reagan on nuclear arms: namely, to treat terrorism as a problem shared by both superpowers and to cooperate, wherever possible, to eliminate the threat. This is in keeping with Mikhail Gorbachev's call in 1987 for "a radical strengthening and expansion of cooperation among states in eradicating international terrorism" and with similar statements from the U.S. government.

Until recently, Soviet experts usually looked at international terrorism through the prism of national liberation movements. Although this attitude has now changed, Soviets often felt that specific acts of terror were "correct." For example, virtually all Soviets believe that any tactic whatsoever was completely justified in the fight against the Nazi occupation; that few people in the West can even faintly imagine the extent of suffering, privation, and humiliation Soviets endured during World War II; and that when Soviet partisans, paratroopers, or secret agents carried out sabotage or murdered German soldiers, these were fitting acts of revenge and causes for rejoicing.

During World War II, the United States backed resistance groups that used similar tactics against the Nazis, and few Americans would disagree with the correctness of this policy. In the postwar years, both East and West continued to support liberation movements that at times used terror tactics.

Looking back on the Cold War, we do not believe that our two nations were equivalent or acted for similar reasons. Nor do we think that Soviets and Americans will ever agree on what happened during the Cold War—on who did what to whom; on who was right and who was wrong. Nevertheless, we feel that both countries are less likely to repeat old mistakes if they learn from the past—even when the memories are not pleasant. While friendship and cooperation are essential to the new relationship, true partnership requires moving beyond politeness and dealing honestly with the world as it is—and was.

Prior to the Gorbachev years, the Soviet government condemned terrorism as a whole but focused little public attention on terrorism committed against Soviets outside the USSR. Unlike the U.S. government, which could be counted on to raise a huge commotion when even a single American citizen was attacked, authorities in Moscow preferred to look the other way and "not to overreact" when Soviet citizens were targets. Soviet authorities usually "advised" their media not to publicize such assaults. To this day, authoritative rumors circulate in Moscow about Soviet geologists and other non-political types who after many years still are held hostage in Angola and Mozambique.

In 1985, four Soviet officials were seized in Beirut. After the incident attracted widespread international publicity, the Soviet government, for the first time ever, publicly condemned an act of terrorism aimed at Soviet citizens abroad. A special envoy was dispatched to Lebanon and Syria. Undeterred, the terrorists murdered one of the hostages, raising fears in Moscow that all Soviets overseas would become targets. At this point, according to rumors widely circulated in the West but denied in the Soviet Union, KGB operatives supposedly seized an individual in Lebanon related to the suspected kidnappers and castrated him. Whether or not there is any truth to this story, the three remaining hostages were soon released. Afterwards, Western terrorist experts would talk somewhat enviously of the Soviet "no-nonsense" approach to terrorism.

Before the 1985 events in Beirut, Soviet officials lived under the illusion that international terrorism was not their concern. While a few Soviet journalists and academics carefully studied the terrorism issue and the conditions that gave rise to it, the government devoted little specific attention to it. In fact, the Soviet Foreign Ministry, unlike the U.S. State Department, did not—and still does not—have a separate section devoted to terrorism. The Foreign Ministry has long regarded the subject as an international law problem and assigned responsibility to the Treaty Law Board. Also, there apparently were—and are—no Soviet commando units, like the American Delta Force, especially trained for anti-terrorist action.

In December 1988, Soviet terrorists seized a bus full of schoolchildren in the city of Ordjonikdze and demanded a $3.5 million ransom. While the KGB closely monitored the situation, there was no coordinated, pre-planned response from Soviet authorities. Soviet authorities were not able to draw from data on past incidents that would be routinely available to anti-terrorist efforts in the West. Although the Aeroflot personnel involved did their utmost to cope with the terrorists, they acted intuitively—without ever having been trained in how to react in such circumstances.

In this particular case, perhaps because children were involved, Soviet authorities decided to pay the ransom and provide a plane for the terrorists to fly to Israel. During the flight, Soviet officials maintained contact with U.S. personnel who facilitated communications between Moscow and Jerusalem, which did not have diplomatic ties. When the plane landed, Israeli forces disarmed the hijackers and arrested them. Then, with Israeli approval, a high-level KGB officer flew to Israel and returned the hijackers for prosecution in the USSR. No lives were lost. The plane and money were recovered. The terrorists went to jail. The incident was a model showing how cooperation can work between countries that historically have had very different attitudes toward terrorism.

The United States has long held "first place" as the preferred target of international terrorism, usually followed by Israel, France, and Britain. By 1989, the Soviet Union had climbed into fifth place, according to RAND Corporation figures, and sources in Moscow revealed that terrorist acts had caused the deaths of sixty Soviets in the preceding years. In short, terrorism had become a Soviet problem—and a problem that will probably increase, given the increasing vulnerability of modern society to terrorist attack. Soviet leaders recognized the threat from "techno-terrorist" attacks on computer systems, electric power grids, and nuclear power plants; from chemical and biological weapons; from nuclear terrorism which might involve terrorists seizing a missile from U.S. or Soviet forces and threatening to push the button; and from ethnic and "narco-terrorism."

In addition, under *glasnost*, the Soviet media have given much more coverage to terrorism, which, in turn, has raised general concern. In some Soviet circles, anxiety about terrorism has been by heightened by the possibility that ethnic conflict—particularly Islamic extremism—will lead to increased terrorism.

Today, both superpowers consider terrorism to be an important problem, and both can agree that no matter what happened in the past, terrorism should in all cases be illegal.

Despite their converging views, the United States and USSR are by no means ready to concur on crucial aspects of the terrorism question. The difficulty in the past has usually occurred when the two nations found themselves on opposing sides of the ideological or political divide. In such cases, one of the superpowers or their friends supported "freedom fighters" or "national liberation fighters" whose struggle was opposed by the other. Examples included the Afghan Mujahedin, the Palestine Liberation Organization, the Nicaraguan Contras, the Popular Front for the Liberation of Palestine, the South African National Congress, and UNITA in Angola. Although the United States and the USSR today are increasingly working together to curb regional conflicts, neither superpower is yet willing to cut its ties with every organization that uses tactics that its foes describe as "terrorist."

Given this reality, we still believe that the Soviet and American governments can cooperate against terrorism if they reject the cliché that one man's terrorist is the other's freedom fighter. We feel that one man's terrorist is, in fact, the other's terrorist. Terrorism is terrorism when it involves the slaughter of innocents away from combat zones—no matter what the justification. We believe that, without exception, any individual, organization, or state that is guilty of terrorism should be brought to justice and severely punished in accordance with national and international law.

There have been serious breeches of this standard. Soviets recall the Bransizkas case in 1970 when a Lithuanian father and son killed an Aeroflot hostess while hijacking a Soviet plane to Turkey. Although convicted by a Turkish court, the Bransizkases were soon freed under a Turkish amnesty law. In 1976, they illegally entered the United States and were eventually allowed to stay by a U.S. court. American officials, on the other hand, maintain that the Soviet Union supports and arms nations like Libya and Syria that harbor known terrorists; these American officials state that if the Soviets are serious about cooperating with the United States against terrorism, they will have to put at risk their relationships with such nations.

In the foreseeable future, neither the United States nor the USSR is going to stop fighting terrorism on its own and in collaboration with its allies. We believe that cooperation between the superpowers should be implemented *in addition to,* not *instead of,* any existing counter-terrorism efforts. Such cooperation would build an additional layer of protection against terrorism—and not interfere with existing defenses.

This book has been written by Soviet and American participants in the U.S.-Soviet Task Force to Prevent Terrorism. Only a few years ago, such a group could not have existed in any meaningful way. Today, our successful collaboration in itself represents a model for superpower cooperation.

Although many of the Soviet and American participants enjoy close relations with their governments, the Task Force is in no way official. In fact, the group would not exist if we had listened to U.S. State Department officials who, during much of 1988, actively tried to discourage our first meetings. Our accomplishments—including this book—demonstrate how unofficial "citizen diplomats" can move out in front of their own governments and find agreements that their governments can then adopt.

The U.S.-Soviet Task Force to Prevent Terrorism had its origins at a conference, the "Citizens' Summit," sponsored in February 1988 by the Center for Soviet-American Dialogue and the Soviet Peace Committee. That gathering brought together several hundred Soviets and Americans for five days in order to generate a whole array of new U.S.-Soviet projects. The "Summit" was in essence a giant brainstorming session— an unparalleled opportunity for Soviets and Americans to try to be innovative together.

The two of us, Igor Beliaev and John Marks, were given perhaps the most difficult assignment. We were named co-chairs of the committee whose job was to find solutions to regional conflict. As much as the Soviet-American relationship has improved, we recognized that our nations still had substantial differences in the Third World—from Afghanistan to Nicaragua to the Middle East. We immediately decided that our best chance to make a difference was to identify a single issue on which effective U.S.-Soviet collaboration might be possible. Regional conflicts seemed either intractable or firmly on the official agendas of our two governments. What could unofficial "citizen diplomats" do? After two days of deliberations with the fifteen or so Americans and Soviets who made up our committee, we agreed that terrorism would be our issue.

Somewhat grandly, we named ourselves the Soviet-American Task Force to Prevent Terrorism, and participants signed an agreement to encourage U.S.-Soviet cooperation on terrorism. Among other things, we decided that the Task Force should include former officials, scholars, journalists, and lawyers who were experts on terrorism; that it would meet at regular intervals in Moscow and Washington; and that its members would write this book.

After inevitable delays, the Task Force had its first meetings in Moscow in January 1989, under the sponsorship of our two organizations, *Literaturnaya Gazeta* and Search for Common Ground, with the support of the Soviet Peace Committee. Far removed from the trusting cooperative atmosphere in which it had been born, the Task Force now included one Englishman and twenty Americans and Soviets who were among their country's leading experts on terrorism. While we still maintained we were "private," the Soviet delegation included officials from the Ministry of Foreign Affairs, the Ministry of Internal Affairs, and key institutes within the Academy of Sciences. On the American side, more than half of the delegation were current consultants to the U.S. government on counter-terrorism.

Yet, these "non-official officials" were able to speak—and probe—without having to represent fixed national positions. By January 1989, both the U.S. and the Soviet governments were providing at least tacit support to the Task Force as a channel in which positions could be ascertained and new initiatives tried out—at virtually no political cost. The Task Force provided both a sounding board for various approaches and a means of judging the seriousness of the other side's interest.

In the month before the first meetings, the incoming Bush administration and Soviet authorities gave their tacit blessings and asked for full reports. The week before we convened, the

KGB's Deputy Director, Lieutenant General Vitaly Ponomarev, declared on Moscow Radio: "We realize we have to coordinate efforts to prevent terrorist acts, including hijackings of planes.... We are willing, if there is a need, to cooperate even with the CIA, the British intelligence service, the Israeli Mossad, and other services in the West." A high U.S. State Department official opined that this statement from the KGB was timed to have an impact on our upcoming meetings. Within days, James Baker, the new American Secretary of State, testified before Congress: "We ought to find out whether Moscow can be [helpful] on terrorism and if not, why not."

While this high-level attention gave cause for optimism, Soviet and American participants in Moscow were still skeptical that anything useful would be accomplished. Cold War attitudes die hard, and the idea that the other superpower had something constructive to say about terrorism was new and beyond everyone's personal experience. Both the American and Soviet participants were taking risks. The Americans feared they might appear naive and foolish or that they might be walking into a Soviet media circus. Soviet participants feared American harangues about alleged Soviet involvement in international terrorism. They suspected that even talking with Americans about terrorism would be interpreted by some of their friends in the Third World as abandonment or as a hostile act.

In fact, no one's worst fears were realized, and the meetings turned out much better than even the most optimistic among us had hoped. Polemics were minimized. Contentious statements were regularly listened to and noted, without leading to major arguments. One member of the American delegation was Marguerite Millhauser, an expert not in terrorism but in conflict resolution. Ms. Millhauser was given a mandate by both Soviet and American participants to break deadlocks, and she contributed greatly to the atmosphere of collaborative problem solving that resulted.

Essential to the meetings was the joint understanding that traditional ways of discussing terrorism had led nowhere and that for these talks to be successful, new ways would have to be found to frame the issue. In fact, earlier talks on terrorism never seemed to get past the inability of Soviets and Americans to define terrorism. Given this reality, the Task Force chose not to define who was a terrorist but instead identified certain acts which constituted terrorism. These included:

1. Hijacking or bombing of airplanes
2. Taking hostages
3. Attacks on children or internationally protected persons (diplomats, international organization employees, etc.)

The Soviet and American participants agreed that these were always crimes—never political acts. While far from exhaustive and perhaps unsatisfactory to international law experts, this mutually acceptable approach still represented a basis to move forward. Once the two sides concurred in what they jointly opposed, they could make long lists of steps that the two countries could take to prevent it. Both Americans and Soviets, in effect, were acknowledging that conceptual differences should not stand in way of their two nations working together to stop what both considered to be heinous acts.

This approach involved separating out—or slicing off—areas that were ripe for agreement, while agreeing to disagree on the rest. The Task Force largely avoided the twin pitfalls of assigning blame for past sins or making vague statements about the abstract future. Soviet and American participants were able to find substantial agreement. But progress was *not* made contingent on one government being required to change long-held policies that the other claims support terrorism. The participants accepted that neither country was likely to cease and desist all activities the other finds objectionable as a price for cooperation. Cooperation was to be based on the two nations recognizing that their own national security is best served by collaborating to reduce the common danger.

Soviet and American participants alike were aware that cooperation on terrorism—even among allies, let alone between rivals—would be quite difficult, and that recommendations would be meaningless if they were not ultimately acceptable to both governments. With all that in mind, the Soviet-American Task Force recommended the following:

- Creation by the two governments of a standing bilateral channel of communications for exchange of information on terrorism; in effect, a designated link for conveying requests and relaying information during a crisis.
- Provision of mutual assistance (informational, diplomatic, technical, etc.) in the investigation of terrorist incidents.
- Prohibition of the sale or transfer of military explosives and certain classes of weapons (such as surface-to-air missiles) to non-government organizations, and increased controls on the sale or transfer to governments.
- Initiation of bilateral discussions on requiring chemical or other types of "tags" in commercial and military explosives to make them more easily detectable and aid in investigating terrorist bombings.
- Initiation of joint efforts to prevent terrorists from acquiring chemical, biological, nuclear, or other means of mass destruction.
- Exchange of anti-terrorist technology, consistent with the national security interests as defined by each nation.
- Conduct of joint exercises and simulations in order to develop further means of Soviet-American cooperation during terrorist threats or incidents.
- Joint action to fill the gaps that exist in current international law and institutions.

These recommendations were reported directly to the White House and the Kremlin, and they attracted considerable media attention in both countries. Within two months of our first meetings, in March 1989, Foreign Minister Eduard Shevardnadze and Secretary of State James Baker agreed to put anti-terrorist cooperation on the superpower agenda. By June, the two governments had opened up official discussions at the working level and had reached their first agreements on superpower cooperation to prevent terrorism.

Both Soviet and American participants in the Task Force believed they had contributed to this new collaboration between their governments. All of us were gratified during the summer of 1989 when the Soviet and American governments worked together in a highly successful way to prevent the executions of Joseph Cicipio, an American-held hostage in Lebanon. Indeed, one of our participants, Brian Jenkins of The RAND Corporation, told a BBC interviewer that without the efforts of our Task Force, the Soviet-American cooperation that, in his view, saved Mr. Cicipio's life would not have taken place.

The Task Force was scheduled to reconvene in September 1989 at The RAND Corporation in Santa Monica, California. Both sides recognized that missing from our Moscow meetings had been people with "hands-on," operational experience in counter-terrorism, and such people usually were found in the world of intelligence. Thus, it was agreed that the Task Force should expand to include individuals with experience in their country's secret services. The American side secured the first acceptances from former CIA Director William Colby and former Deputy Director Ray Cline to join the group. A telex was sent to Moscow announcing the new participants and requesting that the Soviets add former KGB officials of comparable protocol rank. The Soviet side brought in retired KGB Lieutenant General Feodor Sherbak, former Deputy Chairman of the KGB's Second Directorate, and retired KGB Major General Valentin Zvezdenkov, former chief of KGB Counter-terrorism. Never before had high-level former KGB officials come to the West and met with their counterparts. The participation of such people indicates the importance the KGB places on cooperating to curb international terrorism.

When the Task Force met in Santa Monica, Sherbak, Zvezdenkov, Colby, and Cline became the nucleus of the subcommittee on information. Their meetings were cordial. Together, the CIA and KGB veterans agreed that, while protecting "sources and methods," their old services should exchange information to counter terrorism. The ex-KGB men made clear that KGB-CIA cooperation would probably result in an increase in terrorist groups targeting Soviets, but they said the added risk was necessary to curb terrorism. They also agreed that neither the United States nor the USSR should provide weapons useful to terrorists (e.g., surface-to-air missiles or plastic explosives).

Ex-CIA Deputy Director Ray Cline, known for his very conservative views, wrote afterwards in *The Washington Post* that before our meetings he had only dealt with the KGB in "an essentially adversarial context." He continued:

> The KGB came to the United States to assure some of those who would understand that, whatever happened in the past, it really wants to exchange information with US intelligence agencies to suppress terrorists now. What they can and will deliver remains to be explored in official channels. But Gorbachev's seriousness of intent was crystal clear. Our private scholars' delegation was getting an official message.

Needless to say, the bringing together of top retired CIA and KGB officials attracted considerable attention in both the Soviet and American media, including an ABC-TV "Nightline" program which focused on our meetings and, particularly, the possibility of CIA-KGB cooperation.

While the media stressed the intelligence old boys, the other participants were, if anything, more active. In all, the Task Force made over thirty recommendations. These included suggestions that the superpowers directly cooperate to free hostages; that the already established U.S.-Soviet nuclear crisis control centers be expanded to deal with potential terrorist use of biological, chemical, and nuclear weapons; and that the United States and USSR cooperate against narco-terrorism by attacking the laundering of drug money, exchanging data on production, smuggling, and distribution of drugs in Latin America and Southwest Asia, and providing aid to front-line countries in the drug war, particularly Peru and Colombia.

Both the Soviet and American members of the Task Force agreed to deliver these recommendations to their governments at the highest levels. Meetings were held in the United States with State Department, Justice Department, and White House policy makers. In the USSR, a parallel effort brought the recommendations to the attention of the Central Committee and the Foreign Ministry. Special attention was given the intelligence recommendations. Generals Sherbak and Zvezdenkov reported them directly to KGB Director Vladimir Kruyuchkov and his senior staff. In December 1989, the KGB formally accepted the recommendations regarding information sharing. Two months earlier, William Colby and Ray Cline personally presented these same recommendations to CIA Director William Webster. Webster was interested, yet skeptical of Soviet intentions. Then, in October 1990, Webster told the Associated Press that the CIA and KGB were sharing intelligence about terrorist threats and that several times U.S. information had been "pivotal" to Soviet preventive action.

As successful as our Task Force's meetings have been, it should be noted that there was an asymmetry between Soviet and American participants. For more than twenty years, terrorism has been a topic of great concern to Americans, and U.S. experts have developed considerable knowledge on the subject. In comparison, terrorism is a comparatively new field for the Soviets. At the meetings in Moscow and Santa Monica, the Soviets listened and learned, and the Americans, to a large extent, set the agenda. While the Soviets acknowledged they have a great deal to learn, it is obvious that they will not maintain for long their relatively passive posture. For this partnership to work in the long run, it will need to be perceived on both sides as equal and mutually beneficial.

In November 1989, René Moawad, president of Lebanon, was assassinated. Our Task Force, while uneasy with the prospect of denouncing all terrorist acts, decided to use this unfortunate event as an opportunity to illustrate our approach and make a further recommendation to our two governments. The joint statement read:

We the undersigned participants in the U.S.-Soviet Task Force to
Prevent Terrorism unequivocally condemn the assassination of
René Moawad, President of Lebanon, and we condemn the use of
any and all terrorist means, no matter what the justification;
We recognize that the U.S. and Soviet Governments share a common interest in denouncing such heinous acts and in preventing
future occurrences of all types of terrorism;
In order to demonstrate that the United States and the Soviet
Union stand together in opposition to terrorism of which the murder of the Lebanese President is only the most recent example, we
recommend that the U.S. and Soviet Governments jointly condemn this act and that, in addition, they coordinate their response
to future acts of terrorism.

The very fact that our Task Force of Americans and Soviets
could issue such a statement, regarding a country where the
superpowers have long had such different priorities, points up
the potential—that exists alongside the danger—of the international terrorism issue. By coming together to curb terrorism,
the superpowers may develop common ground which can be
expanded into other disputed areas. For example, Soviet
members of the Task Force believe that while American participants loudly condemn Palestinian terrorism, Americans are
mainly silent on Israeli state terrorism such as the June 1989
kidnapping from Lebanon of Sheikh Abdul Obeid, a radical
Shi'ite leader. Leaving aside the substance of this particular
issue, it would seem entirely possible that as Soviet-American
cooperation on terrorism increases, Soviets and Americans
will be able to bridge the remaining gaps on such questions.

In any case, opposing terrorism is much more than a superpower problem. It is an effort in which all countries should
join. The United Nations and other international organizations are already actively involved. We regard our work to
encourage U.S.-Soviet cooperation as complementary to and
supportive of other international efforts. Such collaboration
should in no way be seen as an attempt to have the superpowers dictate to other countries how, when, and where to oppose
terrorism.

In fact, we have already produced the first offshoot of our

Soviet-American group by bringing in Western Europeans. This occurred in May 1990, when *Literaturnaya Gazeta* and Search for Common Ground joined forces with Britain's Foundation for International Security to convene terrorism experts from the United Kingdom, Ireland, France, and Italy, along with representatives from the Soviet Union and the United States. The enlarged group followed the framework established for the U.S.-Soviet bilateral meetings, and the Western European and Soviet participants made a long list of recommendations on specific ways to further cooperation. Most notable was an unofficial understanding between participants close to Soviet and Western European intelligence agencies that counter-terrorism cooperation was desirable on a case-by-case basis, and that such cooperation would be independent of U.S.-Soviet efforts.

First in Soviet-American terms and more recently with the Western Europeans, the process we have started has already had an impact well beyond anything we foresaw at the beginning. In our view, the promise of our approach remains enormous. We are committed to moving forward and expanding.

CHAPTER 2

Setting the Scene

BRIAN MICHAEL JENKINS

The idea of the Soviet Union and the United States cooperating against terrorism seemed far more novel when it was first seriously proposed in 1988 than perhaps it does now in the 1990s. The extraordinary events in Eastern Europe and in the Soviet Union itself that have so fundamentally changed political and strategic calculations had not yet occurred—nor had they been predicted. The Iron Curtain still divided Europe. Eastern Europe, on the surface, was still solidly part of the Communist bloc. Gorbachev had pronounced his policy of *perestroika,* but in 1988 we did not fully appreciate its consequences; and we still remain uncertain as to where this remarkable revolution will take the Soviet Union.

From a U.S. perspective, terrorism emanating from the Middle East remained the most deadly threat, as demonstrated by the bombing of Pan Am Flight 103 in December

Brian Jenkins is Senior Managing Director at Kroll Associates and former chair of the Political Science Department at The RAND Corporation. He is the author of *International Terrorism: A New Mode of Conflict.*

1988—the worst terrorist attack on the United States yet. Iran was widely reported to have instigated this attack, but just as often, we Americans had blamed Syria and Libya, two Soviet allies, for sponsoring terrorism. East Germany maintained close relations with the PFLP, one of the most violent Palestinian groups, while in Poland, Abu Nidal, one of the most hunted Palestinian terrorist leaders, reportedly managed his business interests unmolested by the authorities.

Although clearly on the decline, terrorists spouting Marxist rhetoric were still active in Western Europe. Italy's Red Brigades, historically linked by Western journalists to Czechoslovakia, still carried out an occasional assassination. The Red Army Faction still operated in West Germany while former Faction members, as we suspected then and know now, found asylum in East Germany.

In Latin America, U.S.-backed government forces fought Marxist guerrillas backed by Nicaragua and Cuba, who in turn both depended on support from the Soviet Union. And the United States backed Contra rebels against the Nicaraguan government, Mujahedin rebels against Soviet and Soviet-supported government forces in Afghanistan, anti-Marxist guerrillas against Cuban and Cuban-backed forces in Angola, and even an uncomfortable *mélange* of Communist and right-wing guerrillas against Soviet-supported Vietnamese troops in Cambodia.

Why then would the Soviet Union desire cooperation with the United States against "terrorism"—a word that the two countries had hurled back and forth in a propaganda war? And why would the United States have any reason to cooperate with the Soviet Union, which it still saw, if not perhaps as the worldwide director of international terrorism, certainly as its active accomplice?

Perception of the threat became a crucial issue. We Americans knew how we perceived terrorism, but we were uncertain what our Soviet counterparts perceived as the terrorist threat. To allay suspicions that Soviet-American cooperation was being proposed only to serve other agendas, to go beyond mere rhetoric that it was good for all nations to cooperate with one another against terrorism, the two sides had to find common ground—if not a common perception of the terrorist threat, then at least agreement that there was a threat to both, and that neither Moscow nor Washington was the sole source of that threat.

The American approach was typically straightforward. At the beginning of the first meeting, we laid out how the United States viewed the problem of terrorism. The task was not merely one of defining terrorism. There is no precise, universally accepted definition of terrorism. Discussions of definition are invariably clouded by ideological and political differences as well as by different traditions of armed conflict. The word "terrorism" is itself a pejorative term, and can be used for propaganda purposes. By fixing the label "terrorist" to one's opponent, one can gain a political and moral advantage. While scholars try to give precise meaning to "terrorism," political leaders have used the term promiscuously, applying it to virtually all armed opponents.

America's official definition of terrorism reflected its own particular perception of the threat and, as we shall see, that definition at the same time *affected* its perception of the threat. We wanted to avoid polemics and get down to something more fundamental to describe why, and how, we see terrorism as a problem. We hoped the Soviet participants would do the same and they did, eventually, although not in any single exposition, but rather in the form of answers to our questions and in private conversations outside of the conference room. From these, we Americans were able to distill the principal Soviet concerns about terrorism, which turned out to be justified, as subsequent events have shown, and completely different from our own.

The American Perspective

It is not self-evident how we Americans came to devote so much attention to terrorism over the years. Some explanation is necessary. Despite our own revolutionary origins, as a nation we tend to oppose all types of political violence in principle, preferring instead peaceful methods of bringing about political change, which we equate with democracy. Even where democracy does not prevail, we cling, perhaps unrealistically, to the notion of peaceful change. This has not prevented the United States from backing its side in armed conflicts, whether that is represented by the government or by guerrillas fighting against a government.

Americans take a particularly dim view of political violence in democratic societies such as Western Europe, for example, where we see no excuse for resorting to violent means. In the rougher environment of the Third World, we recognize that some governments may be dictatorships, but it is still hard for us to embrace those who express their opposition with guns and bombs.

This is especially so when they use tactics that have come to be labeled as "terrorism," specifically assassinations and bombs detonated in public places where civilian non-combatants may be killed by them—two traditional terrorist tactics that grew out of an earlier era of anarchism—and the more contemporary tactics of political kidnappings, airline hijackings, seizing hostages at embassies. We regard all such tactics as criminal.

The United States has focused its concern on one dimension of this violence, its spillover into the international arena. This happens in two ways: when terrorists cross national frontiers to carry out their attacks, or when they select foreign nations or foreign facilities as targets. We refer to this as "international terrorism."

In focusing our attention on this international component of terrorism, American concerns become more easily understandable. When terrorists do "go international," they have clearly preferred targets. Ten nations account for nearly three quarters of the targets, five nations alone are on the receiving end of nearly two thirds of all terrorist violence. The United States is in first place. Between a quarter and a third of all international terrorist attacks are directed against American citizens or facilities.

There are a number of reasons for this. Many groups that
have used terrorist tactics espouse revolutionary doctrines
that oppose capitalism and identify the United States as the
world's principal capitalist or imperialist nation. Right-wing
extremists also find reason to attack the United States. The
United States is involved in many contentious issues around
the world; the U.S. government is often incorrectly presumed
to have enormous influence over local governments, thereby
making American citizens valuable hostages; and Americans
are everywhere, and thus always a convenient target.

The other countries targeted most frequently by terrorists
are Israel, France, the United Kingdom, and the Federal Republic of Germany. However, the situation changed slightly in
the 1980s. France overtook Israel for second place and the
Soviet Union ascended to fifth place. According to a chronol-
ogy of international terrorism maintained by The RAND Corporation, the Soviet Union was the target of 169 incidents of
international terrorism between 1968 and 1988, including hijackings in the Soviet Union; the figures probably are incomplete. For the most part these have been low-level symbolic
attacks without casualties. Over half of the total fatalities occurred during hijackings or attempted hijackings.

All chronologies agree that international terrorism has dramatically increased over the last twenty years, measured by
the number of terrorist incidents and by the number of fatalities. At the same time, terrorism has become bloodier: terrorists more frequently target people as opposed to property.
There are more terrorist incidents with fatalities. There are
more fatalities. The most alarming trend in the late 1980s was
the increased incidents of large-scale indiscriminate attacks as
terrorists set off car bombs on city streets, planted bombs on
airliners, in airports, department stores, or discothèques, all
actions calculated to kill in quantity.

Terrorist tactics have remained relatively unchanged.
Bombings account for about half of all terrorist incidents.
Hostage taking in the form of kidnapping, hijackings, or sei-
zures of buildings accounts for between 10 and 20 percent.
Assassinations and armed assaults make up the rest. The

weapons employed by terrorists have changed little, the major area of innovation being in the concealment and fuzing of bombs. Terrorists continue to attack the same targets, symbols of nations: diplomats and diplomatic facilities, airlines, businessmen, and commercial property.

In an effort to avoid polemical discussions, researchers at places like The RAND Corporation have tried to define terrorism according to the characteristics of the act itself rather than the identity of the perpetrator or the nature of the cause. According to RAND, an act of terrorism resembles an ordinary crime (murder, kidnapping, etc.) and in many cases would also be a violation of the rules of war. It is carried out by a group for political ends. The members of the group operate clandestinely and do nothing to distinguish themselves from the civilian population. The violence is directed against noncombatants as opposed to traditional military targets. And it is carried out to achieve primarily psychological effects: publicity, fear, alarm.

While these criteria do not eliminate all ambiguity, they enable us to draw some distinctions. Terrorism differs from ordinary crime in its political purpose and in its primary objective. Neither the ordinary bank robber nor the madman who shoots a national leader for some crazy personal reason is a terrorist. Likewise, not all politically motivated violence is terrorism. Terrorism is not synonymous with guerrilla war or any other kind of war, and it is not reserved exclusively for those trying to overthrow governments. The leftist bomber and the right-wing death squad secretly working under the direction of a ministry of interior both use the same tactics for the same purpose.

However, critics charge that this definition is still ideologically biased since it omits the vast amount of terrorist violence directed by governments (often but not always right-wing governments) against their opponents at home. This bias is not the result of the basic definition of terrorism, which makes no distinction between terrorism from the left or right, government terror or terrorism by opponents of government. Rather, it results from the modifier "international." Most government terror is domestic—that is, it is directed by a government of a country against citizens of that country and is usually carried out within that country. When this state terror crosses frontiers, it is counted as international terrorism.

Acts of international terrorism include: attacks on civil aviation such as hijackings, sabotage of aircraft, bombings, and armed assaults at airports; attacks on diplomats and diplomatic facilities; kidnappings and other forms of taking hostages; assassinations; the detonation of bombs in public places; and other deliberate armed assaults on non-combatants. Approximately one half of all incidents we would record as terrorism are addressed in one of the five major international conventions that were mentioned in the 1985 United Nations General Assembly's unanimous condemnation of terrorism. One major area still not currently covered by international treaty comprises terrorist bombings in public places other than diplomatic facilities or aboard airliners.

The difficulty in obtaining agreement on the definition of terrorism, however, has not prevented international cooperation. Those nations that confront similar terrorist problems and hold similar views—Western Europe, the United States, Canada, Japan, and some of the Third World nations—have achieved an impressive measure of cooperation. And wider cooperation has been achieved by avoiding the definitional problem altogether, concentrating rather on identifying specific targets or tactics that all nations can agree should be outlawed—for example, attacks on civil aviation, attacks on diplomats, and the taking of hostages in general.

American concern about terrorism is not driven by the total casualties caused by terrorists which, although often dramatic and always tragic, represent only a minuscule contribution to total volume of violence in the world. American concern is the result of the psychological effect of this violence. Terrorism is calculated to create an atmosphere of fear and it often works. Terrorism affronts basic values. Terrorists deliberately break the rules, particularly in their selection of targets. Violence against innocent victims provokes outrage, anger, demands for strong responses. The intense reaction causes people to exaggerate the strength of the terrorists and the importance of the problem.

The average American citizen considers terrorism to be an extremely serious problem, sometimes even placing it ahead of issues like nuclear war, crime, and drugs. The average citizen also exaggerates the terrorist threat to his own safety.

The U.S. government worries about terrorism for somewhat different reasons than the American public. Terrorist attacks create international crises which are difficult to deal with and almost invariably put government in a bad light: intelligence has failed; security has failed; if the government is unwilling to negotiate to save lives, it may appear callous; if it yields too readily or is unable to strike back, it may appear weak.

Terrorist attacks also create domestic political crises which paralyze the government, divert leadership from other issues, create public pressure for actions that are difficult to take, and sometimes damage the reputation of presidents.

Terrorist attacks can prevent progress toward the peaceful resolution of conflicts—as they have in the Middle East; terrorism can alter foreign policy—it changed U.S. policy in Lebanon; terrorist incidents can provoke military retaliation and lead to greater conflict; terrorist incidents can start wars or give pretexts for starting wars.

Terrorism also poses a threat to democracy by provoking alarm and creating public pressure for Draconian measures, by unleashing reactionary forces. The pressures are particularly acute where democratic traditions are not strong. In some countries, terrorists have provoked military coups.

Terrorists have assassinated or attempted to assassinate important leaders—Aldo Moro, Anwar Sadat, the Pope, Margaret Thatcher, Bashir Gemayel, the president of South Korea. Thus terrorism is a source of political instability.

The United States has also expressed its concern about what it calls state-sponsored terrorism. A number of nations are using terrorist tactics themselves or employing terrorist groups as a mode of surrogate or indirect warfare or as an instrument of state policy. Examples would include the 1987 sabotage of a South Korean civilian airliner by agents of North Korea; various terrorist campaigns financed and directed by Libya against Egypt, Sudan, France, Israel, and the United States; and the Iranian-sponsored terrorist campaigns against Saudi Arabia, Kuwait, France, and the United States. Iran's exploitation of its control over those holding Western hostages in Lebanon provides a splendid example of the successful exploitation of terrorism to serve Iran's policy ends.

Growing state sponsorship of terrorism has serious consequences. It puts more resources in the hands of the terrorists: money, sanctuary, sophisticated munitions, intelligence, and technical expertise. It also reduces the constraints on them, permitting them to contemplate large-scale operations without worrying so much about alienating their perceived constituents or provoking public backlash, since they need not depend on the local population for support.

We may be on the threshold of an era of armed conflict in which limited conventional warfare, guerrilla warfare, and international terrorism will coexist. Warfare in the future may be less destructive than that in the first half of the twentieth century, but it may also be less coherent. Warfare will cease to be finite. The distinction between war and peace will become more ambiguous and complex. Armed conflict will not be confined to national frontiers.

If a state were to openly shoot down the diplomats or blow up the airliners of another state, it clearly would be an act of war and the victim state would have the right to respond accordingly. In sponsoring terrorism, however, the state denies its involvement and makes an effort to conceal its role. Evidence linking a particular terrorist action and a state sponsor is hard to come by. That makes striking back, whether with diplomatic or economic sanctions or with military force, more difficult. It is this very difficulty in responding that renders state-sponsored terrorism a dangerous weapon and a trend to discourage.

Soviet Perceptions

It turned out that we and our Soviet counterparts had quite different perceptions of the threat from terrorism. They had a much more complex view of terrorism than we did. They feared that a major incident of international terrorism could lead to a confrontation between the two superpowers. They feared growing terrorism against Soviet targets outside of the Soviet Union. And they feared growing terrorism inside the Soviet Union itself which, in their view, might come from ethnic conflict, local nationalism, Islamic fundamentalism, or organized crime.

Until recently, the Soviets perceived terrorism as a peculiar Western disease, a symptom of unjust capitalism or a reaction to the West's opposition to the progressive forces of the world. In any case, it was not a Soviet problem. By 1988, that perception was changing. Although we hear less about terrorism in or directed against the Soviet Union, in recent years hijackings inside the Soviet Union and terrorist attacks against Soviet officials abroad have brought the Soviet Union to fifth place in the list of nations most frequently targeted by terrorists. A distant fifth to be sure, but a development that has not gone unnoticed in Moscow. This ranking is based upon Western chronologies of terrorism. At the Moscow meeting, we learned that our figures are incomplete. Soviet participants said that since 1984, sixty Soviet citizens abroad have been killed in terrorist incidents. Obviously, not all of these have been reported. The Soviet participants also referred to several incidents inside the Soviet Union that we had never heard about.

Soviet concerns about terrorism, however, seem to be driven less by past incidents than by fears of what may happen in the future, where the Soviet Union confronts an array of terrorist threats abroad and at home, some of which are of potentially greater consequence than those we face.

The terrorist incidents of greatest concern to the Soviet Union are those that might lead to confrontation between the two superpowers. The U.S. bombing of Libya obviously made a deep impression on the Soviet Union. Although there was no confrontation in that case, the Soviets worry that some future action by terrorists could provoke similar military retaliation against a Soviet ally accused of sponsorship, which could bring the Soviet Union face to face with an angry United States if it tried to protect its protégé. They may also be concerned that American use of force in response to terrorism could simply embarrass them, as it did when we bombed Libya and they stood by and did nothing to help Qaddafi. In either case, they see the United States as far too ready to employ military force, and they are apprehensive about it.

The Soviet Union also worries about incidents or campaigns of terrorism that could lead to wider military conflict. Again, the Middle East furnishes the most likely scenarios. Third on their list of concerns, they mentioned incidents of terrorism that may involve the use of chemical, biological, nuclear, or any other means of mass destruction.

In addition to these alarms, there is a range of potential terrorist threats peculiar to the current situation in the Soviet Union. The American failure in Vietnam dealt a serious blow to America's sense of confidence about its mission in the world and caused concern about U.S. security interests in Asia, but it stopped there. No one in California felt directly threatened by falling dominoes in Southeast Asia. The Soviet failure in Afghanistan is different. Soviets fear that, inspired by their success, American-supported Afghan rebels may carry their fight into the Soviet Union itself. This is one facet of a broader concern in Moscow that a violent form of Islamic fundamentalism will spread to the 50 million Muslims who live in the Soviet Union. At the meeting, Soviet participants mentioned that green banners and portraits of the Ayatollah Khomeini had already appeared in the Soviet Union.

Soviet fears of militant Islam are part of an even broader Soviet concern that the government could in the future confront violent separatist movements among the various nationalities and ethnic groups that make up the Soviet Union itself. This became clear at one point in the discussions when one of the Soviet participants, in the course of listing Soviet concerns, included the Soviet desire that both countries agree not to interfere in ethnic separatist struggles. Asked for clarification, he explained that if a violent ethnic separatist struggle emerged in the Soviet Union, the Soviets would not want to see any outside powers (clearly meaning the United States) interfere—that is, encourage revolt, or support it politically, financially, or with weapons. As we have seen in the months since the 1988 meeting in Moscow, these fears were well grounded.

This raised an interesting policy question for the United States. The U.S. government would not (and émigré groups would not allow it to) cooperate with the Soviet Union in the suppression of local nationalists even under the guise of combatting terrorism. But would we encourage or materially assist the dissidents? And what does support include? Radio broadcasts from Radio Liberty and Radio Free Europe? Private funds from émigré groups?

The Soviet participants also mentioned their concern about drug trafficking, both into and through the Soviet Union, which they said was increasing.

Finally, the Soviets expressed concern over nuclear terrorism, which aroused a certain degree of skepticism among American participants. Nuclear experts in the West are divided on the likelihood of terrorists being able to acquire fissionable material and secretly fabricate a nuclear bomb or steal a nuclear weapon and successfully bypass the built-in devices that prevent tampering. It can be done, some argue. Others counter that it is far more difficult to build a nuclear bomb than those with theoretical knowledge imagine. Some fear, however, that the prospect of nuclear terrorism becomes more and more likely as the world moves toward nuclear energy based upon plutonium.

Researchers who study terrorism are also divided on the capabilities as well as the motivations of terrorism to "go nuclear." A few consider it very likely that terrorists will acquire nuclear weapons by the end of this century, but the majority consider it unlikely that we will see nuclear terrorism in the next decade. If terrorists decide to move into the realm of true mass destruction, something they have given little indication of so far, other weapons, chemical or biological, for example, offer easier routes.

What then drives Soviet fears? Do their analysts consider nuclear terrorism more likely than American analysts do? Have they read and been convinced by the dire forecasts of Western analysts who view nuclear terrorism as inevitable and possibly imminent, and who invariably receive more attention in the news media than those who remain doubtful or agnostic on the issue? Or does Soviet concern conceal a propaganda ploy? Concern about the prospect of nuclear terrorism in general easily becomes concern about the adequacy of security at nuclear weapons storage sites in Europe, a concern that can be channeled toward the removal of existing nuclear weapons or directed against the deployment of any new nuclear weapons. Fear of nuclear terrorism can also be used to support the creation of nuclear force zones, an idea which the Soviets support.

The meeting in Moscow did not provide a definitive answer, but it did offer a couple of insights. The Soviet participants referred to the issue on several occasions without any indication that their perceptions were based upon analysis (not that we should make too much of our own analysis, all of which is necessarily speculative). The increasing portability of nuclear weapons seemed to impress at least one Soviet participant, who said that he heard the United States not only had nuclear bombs that fit into suitcases but that American designers had developed a "nuclear pistol."

Apparently the Chernobyl reactor disaster also had enormous impact on official thinking in the Soviet Union. It is a short step from this disastrous accident caused possibly by human error to a disastrous accident caused by human malevolence. This line of reasoning evidently provoked serious concern and triggered further research. It also should be pointed out that the Soviet representatives at the International Atomic Energy Agency in Vienna generally have been supportive of strict security and safeguard measures. All this expressed concern about the diversion or theft of nuclear material, and the possible sabotage of nuclear facilities, suggests that the Soviet fears of nuclear terrorism, apart from whatever propaganda value they may provide the Soviet Union, are nonetheless genuine.

COMMENT IN BRIEF*

On the whole, I find Brian Jenkins's view of Soviet perceptions quite convincing. There are, however, certain points I feel I must comment on. In the first place, it seems to me that he is not quite right in suggesting that the Soviet participants tried to dodge certain uncomfortable questions. If, however, he did get this impression, here is the perfect place to declare quite openly: we think the threat of nuclear terrorism is absolutely obvious.

As far as the 1986 Chernobyl disaster is concerned, I'd like to add to what Mr. Jenkins said that Literaturnaya Gazeta *recently wrote: it was not only a question of the human factor. It was also a question of defects in the nuclear reactor itself. Those defects were extensively discussed in many Soviet publications. So it's clear that we had no intention of hushing up this aspect of the tragedy. We only wish to stress once again, together with our American colleagues, the threat of nuclear terrorism and its direct bearing on the human factor.*

Then Mr. Jenkins writes that until recently the Soviet leadership labored under the illusion that international terrorism was none of its direct concern. That's right. However, Moscow changed its attitude not in 1988, as Mr. Jenkins says, but closer to 1985.

After that, my American colleague writes that the Soviet participants in the Moscow meeting mentioned several acts of terrorism that took place in the Soviet Union. Quite correct, and we in the Soviet Union are very much alarmed by this. In particular, we still don't know where the terrorists get their weapons. I wonder if our American colleagues could help us find the answer.

---

*American editor's note: Since this last section is called "Soviet Perceptions" and was written by an American, it seemed only fair that a Soviet, Igor Beliaev, be allowed to give his views.

44   COMMON GROUND ON TERRORISM

Mr. Jenkins points to the fact that the Soviet Union is worried about a superpower conflict being accidentally sparked off by a terrorist act against American or Soviet citizens, or by certain U.S. actions designed to punish those encouraging international terrorism. Mr. Jenkins is right in both instances. But there's one thing I'd like to add. We Soviets strongly believe that both the USSR and the USA must under no circumstances let themselves be provoked by international terrorists into a superpower conflict. As far as the Libyan incident of 1986 is concerned, in my view, not everything actually happened the way Mr. Jenkins presents it, and secondly, the Soviet and American governments acted in that incident in accordance with the notions and rules current at the time in Moscow and Washington. Which is yet another example of the difference in approaches and evaluations that existed—and continues to exist—between our two countries.

Mr. Jenkins goes on to review the present situation in the Soviet Union, emphasizing that certain domestic events were largely influenced by outside factors. To begin with, we are alarmed by the fact that the Afghan Mujahedin (or rebels, as he refers to them) are trying to carry the hostilities onto Soviet soil. Would the United States benefit? I don't think so. After all, Washington keeps stressing its opposition to any attempts to dismember the territory of the USSR in any form, whether it be done by Muslims, Islamic fundamentalists, or anybody else, including those living in the USSR. I think the West must show extreme caution in taking any decision to support Islamic fundamentalism, considering that the latter encourages various terrorist organizations in Asia and Africa—which could threaten both Soviet and U.S. interests.

Brian Jenkins writes that the United States does not intend to cooperate with the Soviets in suppressing "local nationalists," even when it's a question of fighting terrorism. However, the way I see it, the Soviets and Americans should do more, not less, to coordinate their efforts in combatting international terrorism.

Now, on nuclear terrorism. We thank our American colleagues for warning us of the growing threat from this variety of international terrorism as a result of recent advances in nuclear power engineering. Our colleagues in the United States believe that we Soviets fear nuclear terrorism much more than the Americans do.

That's true, because we still haven't got over the Chernobyl trauma, so the vision keeps haunting us of what could happen if terrorists in this country or in Western Europe took over a nuclear power station or caused an accident comparable to Chernobyl.

That's probably all I have to add.

Prospects for Cooperation

It is clear that the terrorist problems of the United States and those of the Soviet Union are not symmetrical. American concerns derive from terrorism directed against American targets in the past. Our Soviet counterparts are concerned primarily about the terrorism that the Soviet Union might confront in the future. As the United States defines international terrorism, it reached a high plateau in the mid-1980s; in the last two years, it has faded slightly. Whether this represents the beginning of a permanent decline or merely a temporary lull, we cannot say. Meanwhile, ethnic and separatist violence inside the Soviet Union is increasing. The major terrorist threat to the United States remains external; the amount of domestic terrorism in the United States is minuscule, particularly when compared with the high volume of ordinary crime. At our first meeting in Moscow and at our second meeting in Santa Monica, our Soviet counterparts focused primarily on the internal threats they face.

Differing perceptions of the threat do not rule out cooperation. The United States may seek Soviet cooperation in certain areas; the Soviet Union may seek American cooperation in other areas. We will trade in different currencies, but we must recognize the limitations. The Soviet Union, for example, can do little to deter Third World guerrillas from attacking American targets, and there is not much the United States can do to help the Soviet government defend itself against gunmen in Armenia or Azerbijan. Nor can we make impossible demands as proof of the other side's sincerity. Demonstrating toughness by demanding that the Soviet Union deliver Ahmed Jabril's head or promptly end its economic support for Cuba

may appeal to certain domestic audiences, but gets us nowhere. And while the United States does not seek the dissolu-
tion of the Soviet Union, the Soviet Union cannot expect the
United States to endorse the suppression of those seeking independence. In other words, both sides must be realistic.

Soviet-American cooperation against terrorism in the near
future is not likely to exceed or even equal the level of cooperation that has been achieved among the Western allies. We
must keep in mind that this cooperation is of recent origin and
took years to bring about. The 1977 Bonn Declaration, in
which the leaders of the seven major Western industrial nations bound their governments to cooperate against terrorism,
was regarded by many critics as empty rhetoric, evidence of
their failure to achieve more meaningful cooperation. At the
1980 Council of Europe meeting on terrorism, Italy complained that French authorities paid little attention to Italian
terrorists vacationing on the Riviera, Spain complained that
Basque terrorists found asylum in southwestern France, and
German authorities complained that French intellectuals, and
sometimes French authorities, were openly sympathetic toward members of Germany's Red Army Faction. France responded that "historical circumstances"—a thinly veiled re-
minder that Italy, Spain, and Germany had all once been
fascist powers—made it difficult for a country with France's
longer democratic history and tradition of giving asylum to
political refugees to take the action the other government
wanted. In 1986, the United Kingdom had difficulty mobilizing other members of the EEC to join it in imposing sanctions
on Syria as punishment for its direct involvement in terrorist
operations on British soil. And in that same year, American
officials were so upset with Europe's lack of cooperation
against terrorism that some politicians suggested that American tourists stay away from Europe, not just for safety's sake,
but to punish Europe economically. One American senator
went further and suggested that America's commitment to
NATO be reduced to the level of Europe's willingness to cooperate with the United States in combatting terrorism.

As recently as 1990, there have been complaints in the

United States that some of the European governments betrayed multilateral pledges to make no deals with terrorists in
order to obtain the release of their own citizens who were held
hostage. (This criticism was only temporarily muted by the
revelation in 1988 that the United States had been making its
own deals for the return of American hostages. Following the
revelation, the United States quickly got back on the no-deals
wagon and again began criticizing others.) As one diplomat
put it, hostage negotiations are a dirty business where it is
every nation for itself. In sum, it has taken the Western nations more than ten years to arrive at the current level of
cooperation, and there are still sharp disagreements, a fact
that should limit expectations regarding Soviet-American cooperation in this contentious area.

Effects on Terrorism

Soviet-American cooperation, at the levels we can imagine,
will not suddenly alter the face of international terrorism, but
it could have subtle and important effects. The Middle East,
where the Soviet Union and the United States have both com-
peting and overlapping interests, remains the most dangerous
area from the perspective of both Moscow and Washington.
The Soviet Union did play a useful role, which is recognized,
in persuading PLO Chairman Yasir Arafat to renounce terrorism, and in getting the leaders of some of the Marxist-oriented
hard-line groups within the PLO to accept his decision. But
Arafat's declaration has not ended all terrorism by Palestinian
extremists, and in June 1990 the U.S. government suspended
its direct talks with the PLO, which were supposed to have
been the reward for renouncing terrorism, because Arafat
would not denounce or punish the leader of a faction that had
carried out a terrorist attack. How the Soviet Union and the
United States might cooperate if faced with a resurgence of
Palestinian terrorism remains an interesting area to explore.

Ironically, the unanticipated events in Eastern Europe have
achieved what some had hoped to have been the result of

Soviet-American cooperation. The fall of Communist governments in Eastern Europe has ended the easy passage of terrorists from the Middle East. But even before the changes in
Eastern Europe, there were intriguing reports that Middle
East terrorists no longer felt secure traveling in the Soviet
Union or Eastern Europe as they feared betrayal by the authorities.

The Soviet Union's increasing attention to its domestic
difficulties has left its Middle East allies like Syria without the
assurance of Soviet protection. This appears to have per-
suaded Syria, and perhaps Libya as well, to mend their relations with the West, which in turn makes the support of
groups engaged in terrorist campaigns directed against or
waged in the West a greater liability. So much to the good. At
the same time, it means that the Soviet Union's ability to moderate the behavior of these states is reduced. Feeling aban-
doned and vulnerable may also increase their ambition to acquire their own strategic weapons and lead to reckless
behavior.

The Soviet Union also played a useful role in the summer of
1989 when it, along with other nations, may have helped to
persuade hardliners in Iran and their protégés in Lebanon not
to go through with the threatened "execution" of a second
American hostage, which almost certainly would have triggered a tough American response. Difficulties in the Soviet
Union have also deprived Tehran from playing a "Soviet
card" against the West, which may give the more pragmatic-
minded leaders in that capital another reason to repair relations with the West, which in turn requires freedom for the
hostages still held in Lebanon. The Soviet Union, having suf-
fered its own hostage crisis in Lebanon, may be helpful here as
well.

These are the results of efforts at the diplomatic level,
which nonetheless have an impact on terrorism. As for more
direct forms of cooperation in combatting terrorism, one of
the most obvious and the most sensitive has to do with intelligence. It is not likely that either side is ready to open its files to
the other—no intelligence service does that—but limited co-

operation is possible under certain conditions, for example, a terrorist crisis involving one or both nations. Participants at the meetings recognized, however, that whatever advantage the Soviet Union may have in access to certain groups is being lost as these groups foresee the possibility of greater Soviet-American cooperation.

Soviet-American cooperation still can be particularly useful in dealing with the more remote but horrendous possibility of terrorists acquiring weapons of mass destruction. Here is a case where the nature and magnitude of the threat will override political differences. Cooperation will be possible to the extent that the machinery for cooperating—communications, procedures, experience in working together—has been set up in advance. This cooperation need not be confined to threats of mass destruction but could also be used in lesser but more likely international crises such as airline hijackings.

Another area where the two nations are already working together and may be able to do more is in combatting the narcotics traffic. The United States has more experience in dealing with addiction (to drugs as well as alcohol). Information on the drug traffic can also be shared to a limited extent. Difficulties will arise in those areas where the traffic in drugs is intertwined with local political conflicts.

As for the direct benefits of Soviet-American cooperation to the Soviet Union in dealing with growing domestic political violence, these are more difficult to see. The United States will do all it can to protect Soviet officials against possible terrorist attacks in the United States, but is very limited in what it can do to deal with any problem of violence inside the Soviet Union.

In sum, Soviet-American cooperation certainly does not end a complex phenomenon like terrorism, but it does offer the prospect of improvements in specific areas. How this might be achieved is the goal of our continuing dialogue.

CHAPTER 3

Terrorism in the Middle East—American and Soviet Perspectives

GEOFFREY KEMP, AUGUSTUS RICHARD NORTON, AND ANDREY SHOUMIKHIN

T he Middle East is not the only region of conflict where short tempers, long memories, and irreconcilable claims spur vicious acts of political violence, including terrorism. But, in contrast to many other parts of the world, the Middle East is the one region where eruptions of violence are almost certain quickly to engage both the United States and the Soviet Union. Both states have major geopolitical stakes in the Middle East, and close ties with the likely antagonists in any serious conflict. Whatever their goals in the region—and there

Geoffrey Kemp is a Senior Associate at the Carnegie Endowment for International Peace; he was formerly Special Assistant to the President for National Security Affairs and Senior Director for Near East and South Asian Affairs, National Security Council.

Augustus Richard Norton is Professor of Political Science at the Department of Social Sciences, U.S. Military Academy; he is the author of *Amal and Shi'a: Struggle for the Soul of Lebanon,* and senior editor of *Studies in Nuclear Terrorism* and *The International Relations of the PLO.*

Andrey Shoumikhin is Department Head, USA and Canada Institute of USSR Academy of Sciences, and a Middle East expert.

is no reason to presume that either aspires to be enmeshed in a Middle East war—each of the superpowers is vulnerable to the manipulation of regional actors.

Simply because they happen in the Middle East, terrorist acts which would otherwise pass with little more than cursory notice in Moscow and Washington are treated at the highest reaches of government. For this reason, and others addressed below, there is a compelling argument for cooperation between the United States and Soviet Union in the Middle East to regulate conflict and thwart acts of terrorism that could precipitate war.

It is a truism, but not to be discredited for being so, that as long as the basic sources of conflict in the Middle East are permitted to fester unresolved, the policies of the United States and the USSR will be a hostage to Middle East instability. Even as the superpowers move toward more amicable relations and inch toward collaborative efforts to achieve an Arab-Israeli peace, there is a troubling prospect that well-planned terrorist acts could be a catalyst for war.

The very fact of improving U.S.-USSR cooperation, which some of the regional actors will perceive as tantamount to an imposed solution, might prompt anti-superpower violence precisely intended to punish the United States and the USSR, to disrupt their cooperation, or to elicit a superpower response. Thus, we face a cruel dilemma: if the United States, Soviet Union, Israel, Egypt and other moderate Arab states, and the mainstream elements of the PLO move slowly toward an historic compromise in the Arab-Israeli dispute, extremist groups of various labels will have an even greater incentive to engage in disruptive acts of political sabotage.

For those who are its victims, terrorism is a nightmare; but for the states affected it is a scourge. Terrorism, per se, does not truly threaten the national security of either superpower or even the Middle Eastern countries themselves, but it can poison relations within and between states and serve as a provocation for war. Terrorism becomes a national security issue, as distinct from a police problem, when it stimulates responses which, in turn, can lead to a breakdown in law and order, create economic chaos, or even provoke interstate and civil war.

Terrorism also tests the will of states that wish to pursue ambitious projections of power. Well-planned campaigns of terrorism were responsible for forcing Israel and the Multi-National Force (MNF) to give up their objectives in Lebanon. The Syrian-backed assassination of President-elect Bashir Gemayel, in September 1982, dealt a mortal blow to Israel's ambition of establishing a friendly government in Beirut. Neither the states contributing to the MNF nor Israel were defeated in strict military terms, but terrorism exposed the lack of domestic political support for operations which were not perceived as vital to national security. As a result, the MNF was forced to withdraw from Lebanon and Israel retreated to its so-called "security zone" in southern Lebanon.

Lebanon is a good case study of the cumulative destructive impact which unending violence can have upon the cohesion of a society. Frequent terrorist attacks by Lebanese on Lebanese have not decisively affected the internal balance of power in the fragmented society. But well-planned episodes of political assassination have impeded and thwarted peacemaking. The November 1989 murder of President René Moawad, for instance, derailed the implementation of the widely supported Ta'if accord.

In contrast, when used against a strong state within its own boundaries, terrorism may do no more than evoke anger and strengthen counter-terrorist operations. For instance, the cross-border raids by Palestinian guerrillas and terrorists into Israel have done little to threaten the State of Israel. In fact the attacks have strengthened the determination of the Israelis to take whatever forceful action may be necessary to prevent them, including some patently indiscriminate military operations.

There are, however, certain scenarios, particularly in the Arab-Israeli conflict, where specific terrorist acts could be the trigger for major widespread conflict. Two examples suffice to illustrate the dangers. In 1984, an elaborate plot by Jewish extremists associated with Gush Emunim to destroy the Dome of the Rock mosque was discovered and prevented only hours before it was to be carried out. The subsequent trial of the conspirators revealed the extent to which the passions of religious extremists could be channeled in disastrous directions.

The Dome of the Rock is the third most revered site in Islam and the most visible symbol of the Muslim presence in Jerusalem. If a plot to destroy it was carried out successfully by Israeli extremists, the consequences would be severe. Given the heightened salience of Islam in the contemporary Arab world, the popular reaction would raise passions that even the most authoritarian governments would ignore only at their peril. The call for a holy war against Israel would be deafening. It is doubtful whether countries like Egypt could resist the pressure to break relations with Israel. Inevitably, some form of counter-violence against Israel would ensue— the downing of an airplane, the blowing up of buses, the use of chemical weapons—not withstanding the likelihood of a harsh Israeli response.

Furthermore, the identities of perpetrators and victims could easily be reversed. Suppose the initiators were not Israelis, but Arab extremists determined to undermine the peace process. Imagine they managed to kill a large number of civilians or destroy a residential settlement with a devastating explosive device. The Israeli response itself would have to be violent and dramatic. Suspicion would immediately be aroused about the involvement of Israel's enemies, such as Iraq and Syria. Israeli extremists, anxious to take revenge, might vent their anger upon the most visible symbols of the Arab presence in Israel, the revered mosques of the Old City. Under such circumstances, the passions unleashed on both sides would be difficult to contain. It would require the most extraordinary diplomacy and forbearance on the part of Moscow and Washington to remain aloof from such a conflict. Whether the superpowers intervened unilaterally or bilaterally to quell the crisis, they would have their work cut out for them. Both would find it difficult to resist the entreaties of their regional clients to provide support.

The problem, of course, is that once major violence occurs

between Israel and its neighbors, the prospect of full-scale war looms quickly on the horizon. New military technologies, especially surface-to-surface missiles, and prevailing military doctrines increase the prospect for preemptive warfare. Warfare this time would be accompanied by missile exchanges, chemical attacks, and possibly even the use of nuclear weapons. These unsavory facts make the formulation of the superpowers' response an issue of high drama and profound importance.

For these reasons, practical cooperation between the superpowers to rein in extremists on all sides of the Arab-Israel conflict must be given high priority. Of course this depends, first and foremost, on a shared conception of what terrorism is and is not. There does seem to be a willingness on both sides to accept the principle that there are some forms of violence that are simply beyond the pale.

The problem with much of the discussion on terrorism is precisely that statesmen, editorial writers, and scholars too readily accept the shopworn cliché that one man's terrorist is another man's freedom fighter. If we use the term "terrorist" with the care and consistency that is warranted, one man's terrorist will simply be another man's terrorist.

The term is a moral indictment that loses its force unless it is used with consistency. This means both sides need to avoid the temptation to label acts of which we disapprove as "terrorism," while turning a blind eye to equally contemptible acts carried out by friends or for goals of which one side or the other approves. Terrorism is not unique to the present era, nor is it practiced only by one's enemies; it is certainly not monopolized by one or another ethnic or religious group.

It is important that moral indictment incurred by acts of terrorism should not be debased or made dubious by affixing the terrorism label to an unjustifiably broad range of events. The tendency to call all forms of violence of which one disapproves "terrorism" is of more than passing concern. Unless the term is used with consistency and even precision, efforts to address the problem will only be met by international skepticism. Of course, "terrorism" is a marvelous epithet with which to bludgeon one's adversaries, but the temptation to label every violent action of an adversary as such is not really a prudent way to build superpower cooperation or to gain wider support in the campaign against terrorism.

Terrorism is the violent targeting of innocents for the aim of achieving a political purpose. Terrorism is opprobrious by definition because of the innocence of its victims and the purposefully indiscriminate quality of its techniques.

An obvious patent example would be the anonymous car bomb exploded on a crowded shopping street in Beirut. No political cause can claim justification for such an act. Other examples include the random shooting of civilian passengers in an airport departure lounge, the intentional mid-air bombing of a passenger plane, or the intentional slaughter of children or other non-combatants. In each of these examples it makes little difference where the incident occurs, what the nationality of the victims may be, or whether the perpetrator was a state or non-state actor. Each case is transparently clear. Naturally, it is possible to conceive of complicating factors which cloud moral claims, but many acts are outright terrorism precisely because such complications do not exist.

Nineteenth-century examples notwithstanding, modern terrorists do not willingly don the label "terrorist." In fact, they go out of their way to avoid it. States which sponsor opprobrious violence disclaim their sponsorship, not just because of the risk of retaliation, but to avoid condemnation.

Not only is terrorism unjustifiable on moral grounds but on practical grounds as well. The cost of terrorism is severe, and not just for its immediate victims. Frequently, the ethnic, religious, or political group from which the perpetrators emerge pays a high price. Consider the unflattering stereotypes of the Shi'i Muslim or the Palestinian Arab communities which are projected by the media throughout the United States, and much of Europe. In Lebanon, the kidnapping of foreigners and other acts of terrorism has provoked a backlash among the Shi'a, who resent being typecast as "terrorists." Just as important is terrorism's contagion effect: it breeds contempt for limits and it inspires imitation. Some officials even argue that terror is the appropriate response to terrorism, so counter-terrorism may literally be counter-*terrorism*.

Terrorism is always unjustifiable. To put it plainly, terrorism is a form of political violence that stands by itself by virtue of its patent indefensibility. The tactic of terrorism is unacceptable, no matter who does it and no matter what the cause. In other words, no end may be allowed to permit the use of the tactic of terrorism. This must be an absolute and incontrovertible stance, for otherwise we find ourselves falling on our own slippery language.

The dialogue between the United States and the USSR has implicitly focused on the non-state actor. But what about the state? The fact that less may often be done about the actions of states—given an international system biased in favor of state—should not preclude an explicit moral indictment of states which practice or sponsor opprobrious political violence, whether they be ally or foe.

Terrorism is not so much an extension of popular struggle as a substitute for it. Popular struggle has a tendency to invalidate terrorism as a tactic. The *intifadah* cannot be called terrorism, nor can the battles between Israelli-backed militiamen and their opponents in South Lebanon. It is noteworthy that Sheikh Obeid, the Shi'i cleric kidnapped by Israel in 1989, played a leading role in al-Muqawamah al-Mu'minah (the Believer's Resistance), which has arguably been more successful than any other group in resisting the "security zone" established by Israel in southern Lebanon.

One can disagree about the wisdom of a given action, yet Israel's use of violence to protect itself is also justifiable, so long as its response is proportionate to the threat. Warfare has rules, and though these rules will necessarily fail to make warfare anything less than horrific for its victims, it is widely accepted that without rules war would be even more horrendous. As a minimum we must insist that what is disallowed in warfare—specifically and especially the intentional targeting of civilians—must be disallowed outside the context of the war zone.

The Soviet Union now recognizes the fundamental moral

fact that terrorism is a crime against humanity. This is but one dimension of the extremely important period of change affecting the Soviet Union's internal and external policies. Both are now conducted taking into account the imperatives of human survival. According to the new Soviet thinking, the parochial interests, be it of a group, class, or a nation, should be secondary to the interests of humanity, and civilization at large. Hence a serious attempt is being made to take ideology out of these policies, and to make them less dependent on narrow sterotypes, self-serving prophecies, and egotistic ambitions.

Critical analysis of the USSR's history leads to a more somber and realistic Soviet view of the rationale behind big power zero-sum games in the Third World, the advantages and disadvantages of patron-client relations, the intricacies of socio-political processes in developing countries, and the effects of their "streamlining" according to specific ideological formulae.

Cardinal changes appear in evaluating the so-called national liberation struggle, its means, methods, and purposes, including the use of force and violence in pursuit of national, social, political, and other goals. To a great extent these changes come out of a philosophical and political discussion of the true meaning of non-interference in the internal affairs of other states, and the right of peoples to make a free choice concerning their social organization and development.

There is also a considerably increased Soviet emphasis on international mechanisms and methodologies of conflict resolution, and a renewed belief in joint international and peaceful means of solving global problems, including the problem of violence.

On top of all this comes a dramatic shift in Soviet attitudes toward individual human rights. An attempt is under way in the USSR to assure primacy of law in internal life, to create a legal system that would put a private individual in the center of all public affairs and would guarantee human rights and freedoms against any abuse by the state. The USSR has declared its readiness to support movements for protecting human life against natural and man-made afflictions, *terrorism included.*

As with any novel concept, the new Soviet thinking will take time to penetrate the realm of practical politics. However, there are already ample examples of how Soviet behavior has been affected by this thinking, particularly in the Middle East.

Soviet withdrawal from Afghanistan was predicated on the admission of erroneous assumptions about the internal conflict in that country and the possibilities of influencing its outcome from the outside. Realism and pragmatism got the upper hand over the illusory ambition to prove that "a superpower is always right."

The USSR played a positive role in bringing the Iran-Iraq conflict to an end. Moreover, in the final stages of the conflict it played a constructive role, when invited, in providing safety for navigation in the Persian Gulf. Like the United States, it acted to inhibit violent attacks intended to undermine international law and order.

Soviet diplomacy also played a significant, if unadvertised, role in bringing about a more moderate Palestinian position on Middle Eastern settlement. Specifically, in all recent contact with its Arab counterparts the Soviet side stressed the importance of political rather than violent military means of resolving the Arab-Israeli conflict.

This Soviet position on the use of force and political violence, including terrorism, contrasts with its earlier positions, which were not uniform and were also affected by conflicting factors, both objective and subjective.

Soviet experience with terror in the Middle East has a complex background. First, there have been cases when Soviet nationals were victimized by terrorist acts inside the region. Second, there is a history of terrorist incidents originating on Soviet territory but destined to reach a conclusion in neighboring Middle Eastern countries. Third, there were instances when the Soviet Union was accused of allegedly supporting and thus being involved, if only indirectly, in activities of terrorist groups in the region. Fourth, certain acts of terror in the region threatened to unleash a major international crisis that could directly or indirectly affect the USSR's security and other interests, and particularly its relations with the United States.

In situations when life or property of Soviet citizens was imperiled, Soviet official and public reaction was always prompt and clearcut. The same goes for hijackings, extortions, murderous assaults, and so on, aimed at Soviet aircraft, embassies, and missions. Every such incident led to strong protests and in most cases to action in order to achieve a redress: the return of hijacked planes and crews, freeing of hostages, and, as far as possible, bringing the perpetrators to justice.

In contrast, until recently, when other states were the targets, the Soviet response was not always as consistent. In an atmosphere of Cold War rivalry, and a strong belief in the virtues of the national liberation struggle, it was not unusual for certain violent acts to be presented as more or less legitimate, or, at least, unavoidable. The blame for their taking place was said to be borne solely by those who indulged in the "suppression and exploitation of peoples."

Ambiguity and complacency on such matters allowed those who were clearly not among the Soviet sympathizers to go on disseminating rumors about "Soviet support" of terrorism. But even in the 1970s, shifts began to occur in the Soviet attitude toward violence and terrorism. Under *perestroika,* these shifts were finalized and reflected in official policy. Two elements played a major role in this connection.

One was a rapid proliferation of terrorist activities in the world, particularly in the Middle East. Terrorism was acquiring a more and more indiscriminate character as all states, regardless of their ideological and political stance, began to suffer more often from the rampant violence engendered in the region.

Another was the policy of detente when a clash or conflict with the United States over a particular violent episode by a certain regime or group could threaten delicate agreements on vital issues of bilateral relations.

A new understanding began to emerge of the human dimensions of terrorism, which required special procedures both on the national and international levels. Two comparatively recent terrorist episodes involving Soviet citizens are illustrative. In March and December of 1988, terrorists struck twice in the USSR. Their methods—the taking of innocent hostages, and demands for them to be allowed to escape abroad—were similar. Most significantly, however, both situations were handled quite differently from a conceptual and practical point of view.

In March 1988 the Ovetchkin family, consisting of a mother and her ten children, hijacked a plane on a regular flight from Irkutsk to Leningrad and demanded to be flown to Finland. Almost without any discussion authorities opted for the use of counter-force and, having landed the plane on a military airfield near Leningrad, stormed the aircraft. In the shootout and a bomb blast that followed, nine people, including some of the passengers, were killed, sixteen were wounded, and the plane itself was completely demolished.

What matters is not only that the operation to foil the hijacking was poorly executed (for example, while landing, supposedly in Finland, the Ovetchkins saw soldiers hurriedly taking military insignia off their uniforms and preparing for an attack), but also that the political decisions to deal with it were wrong.

Acting in accordance with years-old administrative "instructions" that forbade hijacked planes to leave national airspace under any circumstances, those responsible in the Aviation Ministry and elsewhere never thought about the lives of passengers and crew on board the TU-154 airliner (serial number 85413). After the tragedy they did their best to cover up for their incompetence and blind zeal in following "instruction." However, a thorough investigation, undertaken by *Ogonyok* magazine in the best traditions of *glasnost* (No. 26, June 1989, pp. 17–18), exposed the cover up and led to public uproar.

In December 1988, a busload of children were abducted in the city of Ordjonikdze by a gang of criminals. Contrary to what happened in March, they were allowed to fly to Israel after the release of the hostages, in return for millions of rubles and the right of free passage out of the country. Upon arrival in Israel the perpetrators were captured and promptly extradited to the Soviet Union, making the whole international anti-terrorist operation a perfect success.

The Soviet authorities were obviously acting in quite a different spirit in the second incident. Thinking first of the lives of innocent victims and the possible public reaction inside and outside the country, the blunt use of force was put aside in favor of a more sophisticated and enlightened response. Out-of-date procedures were wisely not permitted to preclude it.

What makes this December 1988 episode especially valuable for the study of anti-terrorist methodology is that terrorists were allowed to flee to a country with which the Soviet Union did not have diplomatic relations at the time of the incident. What is more, the Israelis acted in a way that again should go into textbooks as a perfect example of a nation rising above narrow self-interest in the overwhelming and general desire to eradicate terrorism on the basis of international cooperation. A commendable lesson was taught, both for would-be perpetrators of terrorist acts and for political and law enforcement authorities in countries afflicted with the malady. Moreover, cooperation of the Israeli authorities also contributed significantly to the warming trend in relations between Moscow and Tel Aviv.

However, even in the latter operation a few uneasy questions remain. What would have happened if the Ordjonikdze incident had taken place at a time when the USSR and Israel did not maintain consular relations which allowed them to communicate efficiently? What if Soviet hijackers, or at least some of them, were Jewish and claimed political asylum in Israel? What if the Soviet plane arriving in Israel had a few hostages? Who would have been responsible for their rescue?

Therefore we come back to the same set of problems: What, if any, should be the international rules of handling of these and other Middle East-related terrorist actions? What are the ways of establishing permanent international structures in fighting terrorism? Are they at all possible in a context when certain states have no official relations, or worse, are in a clash with each other over other issues, some of which may look even more important than the issue of terrorism? What kind of sharing of information and cooperation in anti-terrorist techniques is possible under the conditions that are common for the Middle East?

All of these questions have to be answered in time. One thing is clear, however: without internationalizing the effort to fight terrorism in the future, the chances for success will be slim indeed. Moreover, in a situation where terrorist groups are expanding their activities, both vertically and horizontally, the time factor becomes very important in providing for an internationally coordinated response to this challenge.

The controversial situation over the hostages in Lebanon that began to evolve in August 1989 in connection with an Israeli seizure of Sheikh Obeid confirms this argument. Israel was clearly on its own in planning and executing the operation. It also had a unique rationalization for going ahead with it, a rationalization not shared by other states concerned with terrorism in the region.

The purported Israeli premise was that a deadlock over a particular hostage situation (three Israeli soldiers were thought to be in the hands of Lebanese Shi'is at the time of the raid) could be broken by force. The Israelis may also have concluded that responding in kind to Shi'i militants would deter further acts of violence.

Practically from the very beginning the "eye for an eye" approach failed, especially when the militants lashed back by allegedly murdering one of their American victims (Marine Lieutenant Colonel William R. Higgins). What is more, other nations were becoming progressively involved in the situation and their reactions were at variance with Israeli thinking and behavior. Rather than winning praise, the abduction of Sheikh Obeid earned Israel sharp criticism in Washington, where its exploit was viewed as jeopardizing efforts to free the Western hostages held in Lebanon. Thus it was again proved that a totally unilateral approach to fighting terrorism, no matter how daring, could not bring final relief but would only exacerbate matters.

Numerous commentators on the incident emphasized the prudent position of the Bush administration and contrasted it with the way its predecessors tried to handle similar situations. No less importantly, the United States opened up lines of communication with foreign governments, including the USSR and Iran. Characteristically, in the new context, the Soviet response was positive and forthcoming. Foreign Minister Shevardnadze made it a point to discuss the hostages with Iranians on more than one occasion, including during a visit to Tehran when he briefly left Paris where he was participating in the conference on Cambodia.

One of the main prerequisites for turning the tide of events in favor of international legality in the Middle East is the growth of mutual trust between states inside and outside the region and cooperation between them on all issues, including terrorism. There is growing consensus that actions to combat terrorism should not deviate from accepted norms of international behavior.

The problem of terrorism is not going to go away, though a combination of prophylactic actions and a defensible ethical stance can clearly impose real limits upon terrorists. Effective cooperation between Washington and Moscow requires that both sides strive to foster an international climate in which those countries supporting terrorist groups will be treated as pariahs. Terrorism must be delegitimized as a tactic. Its perpetrators are worthy only of vigorous pursuit and unflinching prosecution and both sides should act in that spirit. By such means, terrorism will lose its potential to destabilize peace between Arabs and Israelis and between the USA and the USSR.

CHAPTER 4

Religious Extremism–
Links to Terrorism

ROBIN WRIGHT AND IGOR BELIAEV

D uring the 1980s, one of the most chilling trends in terrorism has been the emergence of forces inspired, mobilized, or directed by religious movements. The relationship
between religion and violence is, in fact, not new. History is
littered with holy wars and inquisitions. The words "assassin,"
"zealot," and "thug" derive from fanatic groups that thrived
centuries ago within, respectively, Islam, Judaism, and Hinduism. But violence inspired by or linked to religious movements, a constant in 1980s headlines, had historically been
limited to regional issues and impact. Today, the impact and
the issues are global.

The series of bombings and assassinations claimed by Muslim fanatics in the Middle East in the 1980s were aimed as
much at ridding the region of foreign presence and influence
as at exerting local political pressure. They led to the erection

---

Robin Wright, a former Middle East correspondent, is the author of
Sacred Rage: The Wrath of Militant Islam and *In the Name of God: The
Khomeini Decade.*

of concrete barriers 8,000 miles away—around the White House, the Pentagon, and other key U.S. installations in Washington. Other incidents linked to groups associated with religious movements—ranging from the Catholic Irish Republic Army (IRA) to India's radical Sikhs—have led to unprecedented new security measures costing billions of dollars at international summits, Olympic Games, and airports worldwide.

The emergence of religious-inspired terrorism in the twentieth century is so striking in part because it comes at a time when the world has arguably never been so secular. Indeed, the global political spectrum in the postwar era has been defined by two ideologies notably devoid of religion: the United States is a constitutionally secular society, the Soviet Union is ideologically atheist. Neither, therefore, has been very successful in identifying and dealing with the trend and both, arguably, have been even less successful in combatting it.

The Threat

The deadly litany of attacks in the 1980s by religious-inspired terrorism or motivated groups underscores the impact of the trend: in 1983, two Shi'ite extremists in Lebanon drove bomb-laden trucks into buildings occupied by American and French units of the Multi-National Force. The sophisticated bomb used at the U.S. Marine compound was the largest non-nuclear explosion since World War II; 241 American Marines and 58 French commandos died in the two blasts. Of the more than 140 foreigners from at least 21 nations taken hostage in Lebanon since 1982, the vast majority were believed to be held by religious-affiliated groups, both Christian and Muslim.

The trend is by no means limited to Islam. In 1984, Israel uncovered a network of Jewish extremists linked to car bombings of two West Bank mayors, an attack on Hebron's Islamic College and a plot to bomb the Temple Mount's Dome of the Rock mosque. India's Prime Minister Indira Gandhi was assassinated in 1984 by Sikh extremists, who were also held responsible for the bombing of Air India Flight 182, en route from Toronto to Bombay, which simply disappeared from Irish radar screens monitoring flights over the Atlantic. It had exploded in mid-air, killing 329 people. But both the United States and the Soviet Union feel most threatened by terrorism linked to small cells of Islamic extremists.

For the United States, the threat has always been a long way from home. It originated shortly after the 1979 Iranian revolution, when 52 American diplomatic and military personnel were held hostage for 444 days. Besides the 1983 attack on the Marine compound in Lebanon, two American embassies in Beirut and one in Kuwait were bombed in 1983 and 1984 by Shi'ite extremists. More than eighty Americans and Lebanese died in the blasts. In 1985, a U.S. Navy diver was murdered and thirty-nine other Americans were held for seventeen days in Beirut during the hijacking of TWA Flight 847. There have been a host of smaller incidents, including the murder of two U.S. AID employees during the 1984 Kuwait Airways hijacking, for which Shi'ite extremists have been held responsible. Most spectacular of all was the 1988 bombing of Pan Am Flight 103 over Lockerbie in Scotland, which killed 259 passengers and crew on board as well as 11 on the ground. U.S. intelligence traced the attack to a mixture of Palestinian radicals and an Iranian faction.

For the Soviet Union, the main threat is closer to home. Moscow began to experience the surge of an Islamic identity during its invasion of neighboring Afghanistan between 1979 and 1989 and then within its own borders in the late 1980s. About 54 million people—or 17 percent of the Soviet population—are Muslim and, in the prevailing atmosphere of nationalist unrest and ethnic strife, the threat of new Islamic extremism is viewed by Moscow as growing. In the late 1980s and early 1990, violence broke out in the Armenian enclave of Nagurny-Karabakh in Azerbijan and in the Fergana Valley of Uzbekistan. Religious extremism was not evident in either case, but the presence of the religious factor officially in inter-ethnic politics cannot be ignored. From Moscow's viewpoint, there is the possibility—even danger—of a situation emerging in the Soviet Union where religious problems, and particularly religious extremism, will result in a national crisis.

But the Soviet Union has also had trouble with Islamic extremists in the Middle East. In the 1980s, Soviet advisers to the Syrian government and military were the targets of assassination by the Muslim Brotherhood, a predominately Sunni movement which has unsuccessfully tried to overthrow the regime of President Hafez al Assad. In 1985, four Soviets—diplomats in Lebanon—were kidnapped in Beirut by a Sunni fundamentalist faction. One was killed, the other three were released within one month. Moscow has felt sufficiently concerned by the dangers to its citizens that it has in the past evacuated dependents and civilian workers based in Beirut.

The Background

Like other religious-inspired or directed movements, Islamic extremism did not emerge in a vacuum. As the only major monotheistic religion that provides a set of laws by which to govern a state as well as a set of spiritual beliefs, it is in some ways more prone to political activism in general. Examining the direct and indirect factors that stimulated the growth of Islam as a political force contributes to an understanding of how an extremist wing that conducts acts of violence could emerge.

The first turning point was the 1967 Arab-Israeli War. Until this juncture, two ideologies dominated the governments in the Muslim Middle East, most of which had only gained independence after World War II: the pan-Arab nationalism of Egypt's President Gamal Abdel Nasser and the socialist Baathism of Syria and Iraq. During the two postwar decades, however, neither ideology successfully dealt with the region's growing economic or political problems. The failure was underscored during the 1967 war, when Israel swiftly captured large chunks of Egypt, Syria, and Jordan, as well as East Jerusalem. In six days, the little Jewish state more than doubled the land under its control.

The 1967 war led both Jews and Arabs to turn to their faiths for explanations. Many Jews viewed their overwhelming vitory as a sign from God, and that the time had come for recreation of Ersatz Israel, or Greater Israel, a precondition for the coming of the Messiah. In contrast, Arabs viewed their defeat as a sign they had betrayed Islam. Even Nasser called for greater adherence to Islam after the defeat. The seeds of a revival were thus sown.

The 1973 Yom Kippur War, which also fell during the Islamic holy month of Ramadan, deepened this new feeling. Code-named "Badr" after the Prophet Mohammed's first victory in the seventh century, the Arab offensive was fought in the name of Islam rather than the pan-Arab cause. Although the Arabs lost militarily, their early gains shattered the myth of Israeli invincibility for the first time. They won key political concessions, and the OPEC states' dramatic decision to quadruple the price of oil and boycott sales to the United States because of support for Israel during the 1973 war also gave new power and prominence to the Muslim world.

A third threshold was crossed in 1979 during two events: the Iranian revolution and the Soviet invasion of Afghanistan. In both, Islamic fundamentalists were able to defy the odds of survival. In Iran, the largely unarmed Shi'ite opposition mobilized around Ayatollah Khomeini managed to overthrow the shah and the sixth most powerful army in the world. In Afghanistan, the Mujahedin (Holy Warriors), predominantly Sunni but also Shi'a, not only survived but managed to challenge Soviet military intervention; eventually the Soviets, not the Mujahedin, backed away. Islam was increasingly seen throughout the Islamic world as a powerful idiom of political opposition.

The fourth turning point was the 1982 Israeli invasion of Lebanon and its three-year occupation. Again, Islamic activism, largely among Lebanese Shi'a, proved capable of achieving in three years what the Palestine Liberation Organization had been unable to do for two decades: under increasing attack, Israel withdrew unilaterally in 1985 without security guarantees for either the volatile border or vulnerable northern Galilee—the very reason for its invasion. Islamic extremism, largely by the Shi'a, against the U.S. and French contingents of the Multi-National Force (MNF)—which arrived in 1982 to "monitor" the peace, but which many Muslims increasingly perceived as pro-Christian—also forced the MNF to withdraw in early 1984. By the end of the decade, Islam had become synonymous with victory—even against the superpowers. By the time of the Palestinian uprising in Israel in 1988, few Middle East analysts were surprised by the emergence of fundamentalist factions among Palestinians, traditionally the most secular Arabs.

Certain characteristics about Islam also contributed to the new wave of religious extremism in the 1970s and 1980s. First, Islamic sacred writings are more diverse and even contradictory than Christian scriptures. The Koran contains, for example, both the purely Christian precept "thou shall not kill" and a call to eliminate infidels; the recommendation to spread Islam by the sword as well as an unambiguous statement that there is no compulsion to adopt the faith; the idea of the predetermined nature of human life and the assertion that man enjoys freedom of choice. The Koran also contains a demand that an apostate—meaning a Muslim who rejects Islam—be killed as well as an appeal for tolerance. And the divine revelations to Mohammad include "Say: This is the truth from your Lord: Let him who will believe in it, and him who will deny it," and "As to those who pay no heed to you, know then that we have not sent you to be their keeper." The extremist can thus find justification for his opinions in sacred writings.

Second, the clergy is empowered to interpret religious tenets from the Koran and the Hadiths, the canonized narrative of Islam in its earliest period. The clergy is thus capable of mobilizing followers to action. Shi'ite Muslims are especially prone to this process. While members of the mainstream Sunni sect believe man's relationship with God is direct, the Shi'a emphasize the role of the clergy in intervening between man and God and in reinterpreting the Koran by drawing up guidance for the individual. Ideally, an infallible imam should establish truth for the faithful. In the absence of an imam, other legal religous experts (mujtahids) can independently interpret religious truths. Imams and mujtahids thus have the power to develop doctrines and laws with a highly specific—and even extreme—political content.

The Broader Context

Not surprisingly, the emergence of religious-inspired terrorism, not only within Islam, coincides with the growth of religion in politics generally. Although the United States and the Soviet Union have both witnessed the growth of politicized religious movements at home, the trend is most vibrant and visible in the developing world—the more than one hundred nations ranging from thriving, newly industrialized states to impoverished countries, most of which have become independent only since World War II. Among the recent examples: in 1987 and 1988, Buddhist monks were at the forefront of opposition in Tibet. In the Philippines and Haiti, the Catholic clergy played major roles in the simultaneous February 1986 overthrows of two notorious right-wing dictators, while Catholic Liberation Theology has been a strong political force throughout Latin America in the 1980s. In South Africa, black, colored, and white ministers, such as Anglican Bishop Desmond Tutu and the Dutch Reformed Church's Allen Boesak and Beyers Naude, for years led the anti-apartheid movement in the absence of exiled or imprisoned political figures.

Among the various movements, there are more differences than similarities in flashpoints, tactics, and goals. But the coincidental trend suggests some common themes, particularly in Third World communities struggling in the postwar era to find ideologies and systems that will address deep political and economic problems, or trying to oppose dictatorships or one-party nations in which political opposition is banned. In many cases, the societies also are in transition, attempting to move from perceived impotence to empowerment; violence is seen by a minority as one means to that end.

One of three factors—political repression, economic inequality, or social upheaval—has usually reached crisis proportions in areas where religion has become a political force; ethnic or military disputes are a fourth common factor. During a conflict or crisis, the continuum of various faiths, which have survived centuries and outlived hundreds of political dynasties, offers a vehicle for opposition. Religions provide refuge as well as a set of beliefs by which to seek alternatives and an infrastructure through which to operate. In several areas, religions have become at least a temporary political idiom. The emergence of extremist factions from within some of these politicized religious movements is thus, in many ways, no more surprising than the rise of extremist groups from within secular political movements.

In this changing political climate, religious groups appear to turn to terrorism or extremist violence in one of three situations.

First, minorities, either within a nation or a religion, are more susceptible to mobilization because of perceived threats to their identity or survival. Among the contemporary examples: Sikhism, a monotheistic faith that grew out of Hinduism in the sixteenth century, constitutes only 2 percent of India's 800 million people. Sikhs have long feared absorption by the dominant Hindus. Lebanon's Maronite Christian minority has balked at giving up its edge in government, a key Muslim demand to end the civil strife that has raged since 1975; the various Muslim groups that now constitute the majority have, meanwhile, perceived themselves as the political minority. While much of the violence has been open warfare, both Christian and Muslim militias have also engaged in terrorism, from hostage seizures to car bombings, to promote their causes. Iran's Shi'i are a majority domestically, but the sect represents less than 15 percent of the world's Muslims, and the minority sense of persecution has been a dominant Shi'i theme for thirteen centuries.

Second, increased religious militancy within one sect can heighten consciousness and militancy in others, creating a cycle difficult to break. Sikh and Muslim militancy in India, for example, has led to new Hindu activism. The 1984 Indian Army raid on the Golden Temple in Amritsar, the Sikh's holiest shrine, resulted in more than a thousand deaths. Sikh extremists murdered Mrs. Gandhi four months later, which in turn triggered a Hindu massacre of an estimated twenty-five hundred Sikhs. Since then, terrorism has become a fact of daily life in India's Punjab province, the Sikh stronghold. The emergence of Islamic fundamentalism and extremism in the Middle East since 1979 has been a factor in the rise of Jewish extremism in Israel and the occupied territories, in turn further fueling Muslim fanaticism among Palestinians. In Nigeria and Egypt, Christian minorities have become restive under pressure from Islamic majorities. The worst sectarian strife, which included many acts of terrorism, in Nigeria's post-independent history erupted in 1987.

Third, goals centering on economic, ethnic, or political issues can evolve into disputes over religious principles or dogma and hence become non-negotiable. For example, in Lebanon, the prolonged strife between Christian rightists and Muslim leftists and Israel's 1982 invasion fueled the rise of Shi'ite and Sunni fanaticism. Militant cells and groups now advocate turning the Levant into an Islamic republic, making resolution even more difficult. The Sikh issue became a major political factor in the 1960s with demands for a separate Punjab-speaking province, to which Mrs. Gandhi agreed. After two decades of political disappointments, a militant Sikh council in 1986 proclaimed Punjab to be the independent state of Khalistan or "Land of the pure," and declared holy war on the government.

The Response

The superpowers' response to the emergence of religious-inspired or directed terrorism is most vivid, again, in their handling of Islamic extremism. Neither, so far, has fared very well.

Washington has proved virtually impotent in dealing with

the various groups that have attacked both civilian and official targets—beyond issuing travel warnings and tightening security. Despite the humiliating impact of the 1979–81 hostage crisis in Tehran, Washington was late in identifying the trend. Compounding the error, U.S. officials did not foresee that the tactic might be repeated elsewhere. The two hostage ordeals—in Tehran and in Beirut—turned out to be the single biggest failures for both the Carter and Reagan administrations. The taking of a handful of Americans also led to some disastrous decisions. In 1985–86, the Reagan administration's inner circle contradicted U.S. policy and circumvented Congress in trading arms for three American hostages with Iran. Since then, the Bush administration has tried a carrot-and-stick approach—again unsuccessfully. In his inaugural address, President Bush pledged that "goodwill begets goodwill" in a signal to Tehran to exert influence over its Lebanese allies. At the same time, he pledged to stand firm against any deals with hostage takers. As of early 1990, six Americans were still held hostage in Lebanon.

Its failure was again evident in Lebanon between 1982 and 1984, when the Reagan administration did not foresee the explosive potential of its military deployment—even after U.S. warships opened fire against Muslim militias to help the beleaguered Christian-dominated army. Later, in 1988, in the aftermath of the U.S. Navy's shooting down of an Iranian airbus, which killed 190, the Reagan administration failed to forecast a revenge attack—specifically, on a U.S. airliner such as Pan Am 103.

In 1984 and 1986, Congress passed two tough anti-terrorism laws, which gave Washington extra-territorial rights to arrest terrorists responsible for either hijackings or hostage seizures. But as of early 1990, only one hijacker was apprehended—for the hijacking of a Jordanian plane on which two Americans were traveling. The United States also created counter-terrorism centers within both the State Department and the Central Intelligence Agency in the early 1980s. But each followed the format of other government agencies in dealing with foreign policy; assignments were broken down along regional lines and did not look at transnational trends such as religion in politics. The CIA had regional analysts who monitored, for example, the role of Islamic activism in specific countries, but no facilities or personnel were allocated to correlate the common denominators.

In general, the Reagan and Bush administrations have approached the problem of terrorism from a single dimension: that all acts of terrorism are criminal. While no act of extremist violence against innocent civilians can be condoned, Washington policy makers have been either unwilling or unable to examine how terrorism is also often the by-product of perceived sociopolitical or economic injustice. Religious-inspired political extremism has emerged in situations in which groups believe their rights have been abused, neglected, or suppressed. Counter-terrorist strategy must thus acquire a wider cultural, social, and political dimension if it is to succeed.

This is also true of the Soviet Union to a similar, perhaps even greater, degree. As Moscow reconstructs itself economically and politically, the potential for perceptions of injustice is high. An effective response to the possibility of some Jihad or other religious-based violence is dependent on the eventual definition of a successful policy to deal with the socioeconomic and political problems of ethnic and nationalist groups, including those in Muslim communities.

In response to Islamic extremism elsewhere, the Soviet Union in the late 1980s tightened security precautions, joined international efforts to condemn terrorism, and publicly called for new cooperation with the West on anti-terrorism measures. On the hostage issue, Moscow has had no further recurrences in Lebanon since the single 1985 incident, in part due to its different tactics and its different relationship with the main players. The four Soviets were abducted by a group headquartered in Tripoli, the northern Lebanese port city, which was being besieged by Syrian troops; the group, Tawheed, demanded that the Soviets force Syria to withdraw. A widespread myth that emerged from this incident involved the abduction by Soviet allies of a leading Tawheed member or a relative of a Tawheed leader; he was then allegedly killed, his genitals cut off and stuffed in his mouth, and his body dumped in a public place as a warning to release the three surviving Soviets.

In fact, Moscow dispatched a ranking official to Damascus to discuss the Soviet hostage situation and Syria's involvement in Tripoli. The Soviets also worked closely with their Druze militia allies in Lebanon to find the hostages and pressure their captors. Eventually, terms for a cease-fire—involving the disarming of Tawheed in exchange for an end to the Syrian onslaught—were worked out, and the Soviets were freed. Moscow, however, believes that the possibility of further attacks against Soviet citizens in Lebanon or elsewhere cannot be ruled out. Indeed, the Soviet government today believes it faces the same threat as the United States, Western Europe, Israel, and moderate Arab nations have been since the late 1970s.

The Future

The broader trend implies many current and future dangers for U.S. and Soviet national security interests, particularly at a time of unprecedented cooperation between the two nations on resolving regional conflicts and when internal Soviet ethnic unrest has a clear religious dimension. One of the dangers is that the introduction of religious extremism into a conflict can alter the formula and chances of resolution. Over time, temporal social or political struggles can evolve into disputes on a higher plain, between God's truth and the Satanic evil of the opposition and, in turn, then justify the kind of violence and terrorism that the religions in theory disavow. Even if the religious-inspired extremist faction is in the minority, as all of them were in the 1980s, the potential for each to play the spoiler in any resolution that does not address its extremist agenda is high.

Another danger is that trying to combat or suppress these movements can be particularly problematic since their members are often prepared to die, in marked contrast to the secular terrorist movements that emerged in the late 1960s and 1970s in Europe, Latin America, and the Middle East. Relations between religiously inspired terrorists and secular political movements can often be uneasy. Khomeini supported the Palestinians in their struggle against Israel, but eventually relations deteriorated over PLO ties with Iranian opposition groups. Since 1983, Iran has increased its ties with radical Palestinian factions and religiously motivated fighters based mainly in Lebanon. The greatest future danger for both superpowers is that religious-inspired terrorist groups will pool their resources with hard-line secular groups, as the various European terrorist groups reportedly did in the mid-1980s.

As the United States and the Soviet Union begin their efforts at joint resolution of regional conflicts, as well as the bilateral talks on international terrorism initiated in 1989, the efforts must move beyond a superficial level—namely, exchanges of information on planned attacks or arms acquisitions. While any bilateral cooperation is an improvement over the tension and accusations of support for respective surrogates that has prevailed since terrorism became a weapon of modern warfare in the late 1960s, their joint attempts at curtailing international terrorism must reach deeper into the troubled political environments in which religious-inspired violence thrives.

CHAPTER 5

Narco-Terrorism

VLADIMIR VESSENSKY

Budapest, Hungary–January 1987

The Colombian ambassador, Enrique Gonzalez Parejo, walked out of his house. A man dressed in gray cut him off. "Weren't you once the Minister of Justice in Colombia?" "Yes," answered the ambassador. The man pulled out a pistol and shot five times. Three bullets hit the ambassador in the head. Somehow he survived.

By all norms of international law, this was an act of terrorism. An ambassador—a diplomatically protected person—had been gunned down while serving his country abroad. But this was not political violence of the type generally associated with attacks on diplomats. The motives were based in Colombia's cocaine trade. The shooting was an example of an emerging form of terrorism called narco-terrorism.

A foreign correspondent and editor of *Literaturnaya Gazeta*, Vladimir Vessensky has had extensive experience in reporting from Latin America. He spent the 1990–91 academic year as a Nieman Fellow at Harvard University.

Violence has always been an inevitable part of the drug trade. Until recent years, however, drug traffickers mostly aimed their violent behavior at law enforcement agencies interested in trying to arrest them and at rival gangs with which they competed for profit, territory, and supply. Increasingly in recent years, narco-battles have spilled over into the non-criminal world. Today's narco-terrorism involves assassination of political leaders, bombing of civilian airplanes, alliances between armed guerrillas and narco-traffickers, widespread gunrunning, and no-holds-barred struggles for political control of entire countries.

By pulling off a gangland-style hit on an ambassador in Hungary, the Colombian narco-mafia was demonstrating its powerful outreach. Yet the Western press hardly took notice of this event, which did not fit, at the time, the popular stereotype that the tentacles of Colombian narco-traffickers did not reach into the socialist countries of Eastern Europe.

This kind of inaccurate stereotyping was not limited to the narco-mafia alone. It also could be seen in the American view of how to deal with the drug problem in Colombia and other South American countries. Consider how readily U.S. authorities welcomed the use of military measures—to meet narco-terrorism with counter-narco-terrorism. Yet those same authorities categorically rejected the views of any local politician who dared to propose that illegal drug trafficking be stopped by legalization. I believe that, to a great degree, much of the conflict came out of an inaccurate or incomplete stereotype held by Americans of the problem.

Let's take a look at the origin of the stereotype, starting with some generally accepted facts. It was clear that Colombia, Bolivia, and other Latin American countries produced and illegally transported narcotics to the United States. The Colombian drug mafia supplied an army of dealers who sold narcotics on the streets of U.S. cities, in schools, discos, bars, and other places young people congregate. Narco-producing countries like Colombia were seen in the United States to be largely in the hands of the drug mafia, and these countries were viewed as aggressors; Americans, according to this stereotype, were the victims of aggression. Colombian "aggressors" received multi-billion-dollar revenues from their illegal activities, while the American "victims" mourned their children, friends, and loved ones, who were physically and morally destroyed. This "aggressor-victim" syndrome took on a military tone, and it was viewed as a struggle with evil. But unfortunately, besides measures of force, no effective non-violent solutions were developed.

I asked Dr. Gaston Ponce Caballero of the Bolivian Red Cross whether Bolivia is a victim or an aggressor in the drug wars. He answered, "For the U.S., we Bolivians are all drug traffickers, drug dealers, mafioso." Then he asked, "Is it just because coca grows in Bolivia, because our peasants use coca leaves? Is it really fair?"

On the road to Los Jungas, Bolivia

I am being driven on the mountain pass from La Paz to Los Jungas. The pass is above 16,000 feet. I look down on both sides of the narrow, curving road into the abyss. The city ahead is at about 13,000 feet. People are dirt-poor. Thousands are drug users. Here, "coca" is an ancient, sacred plant. The *conquistadors* found medicinal qualities in it. For centuries, coca has supplemented the diets of Indian peasants. It brings joy and healing. It takes away thirst, hunger, and pain. Indians chew a few coca leaves, and poverty is not so frightening, the wind not so cold.

Before cocaine became the yuppie drug of choice in the United States, Bolivia produced annually only 10,000 to 15,000 tons of coca—not so much considering that 3 million Bolivians use coca. Part of the harvest went to the pharmaceutical industry, part to direct use, and part for making tea (which still is widely available in La Paz and which is wonderful for getting rid of height sickness). And Bolivians were not the only beneficiaries. For many years, the Coca-Cola Company added coca to the drink that took its name from the plant. It never occurred to Bolivians to call American consumers "users." (Maybe this was the start of the double standard.

As Latino author Mario de Andrade wrote, if the white man runs, he is a champion. If a black man runs, he is a thief.)

Turns, and more turns . . . The last time I took this road was in the 1970s. General Torres was in power in Bolivia, and everyone seemed to have hopes for a better life. On the road, there were Toyotas piled high with yucca, bananas, oranges, onions, garlic, pineapples. A family could cash in on a harvest of pineapple to make the first payment on a truck. And with a truck, an Indian could be more than a peasant. Many people shared that hope. "Those times are gone", says Jose, a forty-five-year-old Indian driver. "Coca has destroyed the people who grew pineapples and oranges and even the coffee planters. Coca put everyone out of business." The numbers are simple: a hectare of coca brings $13,000 in revenues; a hectare of coffee, $3,000 to $7,000.

We turn off the road to talk with some farm workers. They refuse to answer our questions. Coca has changed the character of the people. They fear we'll photograph their crops and write about them. Then the police will come and burn the harvest. Further down the road, we see some coca plants, gather a few leaves, and put them in a plastic bag to make tea later. Coca leaves like these must go through a chemical process to become cocaine. Almost all is exported. Without the colossal U.S. market, there would be almost no demand. The essence of the debate boils down to: Who is at fault? The producer or the user?

Unlike the Reagan administration, the Bush administration recognizes joint responsibility. But the Bush policy against drugs is still to use such measures as armed troops, defoliants, and a few million dollars for restructuring the farming economy. But what's a few million dollars in comparison with the untold riches of the drug mafia? Imagine the situation of the farmer whose coca bushes are his sole source of regular income. For a Bolivian peasant, coca is what his father and his ancestors grew. How would an American farmer react if his wheat harvest were to be burned without compensation, because whiskey was being made from the wheat and the whiskey was leading to alcoholism in Brazil? In the countryside, the poor farmers seem to be the real victims of the war on drugs.

A trip back to La Paz prompts another conclusion: In the city, Bolivia looks like the aggressor who profits from cocaine, sells it abroad, and hence destroys the health of whole nations. Walking around the city is like being in a department store. Japanese and Korean electronics are everywhere, sold like cookies from sidewalk stands. Expensive cars zip around the city. Perhaps this sight of comparative riches leads some to advocate the use of force in dealing with the narco-mafia.

In Latin America, however, military tactics are met with suspicion and exasperation. In September 1986, Bolivia made a much publicized decision to let in American armed forces, including 260 U.S. soldiers and helicopters, to help destroy the narco-mafia. Latin newspapers wrote that the goal of the operation was not so much to find secret drug installations as to identify construction sites for future military bases and landing pads for U.S. special forces.

At the same time, another incident seemed to confirm these fears. On September 5, 1986, an airline pilot and a guide flew a famous Bolivian scientist, Noel Kampf Mercado, and a Spanish biologist, Vincente Castello, into the Bolivian countryside on a scientific mission. After they landed, Noel Kampf and the guide started to look around. They soon returned, escorted by two armed men, who then shot Kampf, the guide, and the pilot. The Spaniard managed to run away and hide in a thicket until the next morning. Then another expedition landed. He rushed up to the plane and told them about the murders. They escaped under fire. It is obvious they had stumbled across an underground cocaine factory and its guard force.

The death of one of Bolivia's leading scientists shook the country. A parliamentary commission was formed to investigate. Mario Velarde, who headed the commission, told me, "The lack of technical means impeded the seizure of the factory and the arrest of the leaders of the drug outfit." The Bolivian government did not have the means, but the U.S. government had the necessary helicopters and troops. I learned that the American Drug Enforcement Agency (DEA)

decided it was better not to scare away the big game . . . and
the big game got away, in any case.

Bogotá, Colombia

I'm facing the Palace of Justice. It was once a beautiful
building made of rose-colored marble and glass. Now, it's a
burnt-out shell. The Colombian flag is being used to cover a
bomb hole over the main entrance. In November 1985, M-19
guerrillas seized the palace and took hostage eleven justices of
the Colombian Supreme Court. Colombian troops ringed the
building. No real negotiations took place. Fierce fighting
broke out. Among the many killed were eleven Supreme Court
justices. Destroyed were the files on six thousand drug cases,
including dossiers on many of Colombia's most notorious
traffickers, whose extradition the U.S. Justice Department was
demanding. It was widely assumed that M-19 was collaborating with the drug mafia, and that this was narco-terrorism at
work.

The drug-related violence which has swept Colombia had
its origins in the 1970s when the end of the Vietnam War cut
the United States off from many of its drug sources in the Far
East. At that time, enterprising Colombians set up marijuana
production on the northern coast of the country. The first
barons of the narco-mafia appeared and scored quick riches.
They had so much excess cash that they bought up huge
chunks of land, purchased political influence, built private ar-
mies, and bought newspapers, radio stations, and soccer
teams. In the late 1970s, as illegal marijuana growth soared in
the United States and pressure mounted from the U.S. government to end production, Colombia's drug lords switched
their attention to traffic in the much more profitable drug of
cocaine.

Formed during this period was the so-called Medellin Cartel, whose revenues reached the billions. Using their extraordinary economic power, these cocaine *nouveaux riches* put
their massive profits to work in corrupting the country's politi-

cal institutions. Pablo Escobar, a leader of the Medellin Cartel, was elected to parliament; many of his fellow legislators openly supported drug interests. Another Medellin chief, Carlos Lehter, son of a German emigrant, created a political armed pro-fascist organization. In 1984, in the "neutral" country of Panama, there was an historic meeting between drug lords, on the one hand, and former President Lopez Michelsen of Colombia and Colombia's Public Prosecutor, Carlos Jiminez Gomez. The narco-bosses clearly were interested in acceptance from the traditional governing classes in the country. Among other things, they wanted to legalize their position and to take on more political power. The narco-mafia offered to pay off Columbia's foreign debt of $14 billion in return for amnesty. They said that, if the government accepted, they would stop producing and exporting narcotics and destroy all landing sites and laboratories.

Certain people in the Colombian government thought the drug mafia's proposal had merit. Already Colombia was dependent on drug money to support its economy and to lighten the burden of foreign debt. Opposing negotiations with the mafia were traditional politicians, both conservatives and liberals from the two strongest political parties of Colombia. The American government and press were vehemently against any agreement, and the offer never was acted on. And so the narco-war began. Unable to get its way through negotiations, the drug mafia expanded its use of political murders, bribery, and blackmail.

During the early 1980s, the drug mafia's greatest obstacle to power seemed to be Colombia's Minister of the Interior, Lara Bonilla. This courageous minister had exposed connections between drug traffickers and highly placed officials, members of Parliament, and multinational corporations. In April 1984, Lara Bonilla was gunned down. Investigation of his murder was assigned to the court of Manuel Castro Jille. Disregarding mafia threats, Castro Jille went after the killers. Well-known drug lords were captured by the police. But ultimately, Castro Jille was murdered himself. The killings continued. The vic-

tims of this narco-violence were people who had crossed the
drug lords: journalists, judges, members of parliament, local
officials.

Violence: a normal day in the capital

Bogotá is a city of 5 million people, with tall buildings cutting through low-hanging clouds and old neighborhoods of
homes with tiled roofs. On sidewalks, thousands of merchants
display goods in a way that crowds out the walking space of
passers-by. In the wealthy parts of the city, the rich live
guarded and fenced off from the outside world. But in Bogotá,
even this does not guarantee security. Violence makes itself
known everywhere. The poor quarters are far away, on the
slopes of the surrounding mountains. The disparity in neighborhoods is said to be a principal reason for the escalating
violence.

Each morning I walk from the Hotel Bakata to the news
agency where I work. One day, I take the elevator to the seventh floor and find everyone at the window. Outside, the em-
erald merchants have attacked a man. He is rolling around
with a knife in him, in obvious pain. The police appear on
motorcycles and whisk him away. This is violence seen with
my own eyes, I think. I am struck by the notion that this sort of
scene is mundane to a Colombian.

I speak about the violence with the noted Colombian sociol-
ogist Alvaro Camacho. "A typical Colombian type of violence
is commissioned murder," Professor Camacho says. In Colombia, there are special schools in which the drug mafia
teaches young people to fire automatic weapons and pistols
from speeding motorcycles. The killers are young people,
sometimes minors, uneducated or ignorant, deprived of any
perspective on life. Murder is, for them, ordinary work. The
world of the mercenary killers has its own rules and standards.
They live with one goal—to kill anyone they are ordered to
eliminate: a scholar, journalist, minister, or just a citizen.
Beyond the borders of Colombia it is hard to imagine this level
of violence.

"Tell me," I ask Señor Camacho, "how much does it cost to have someone killed?"

"Forty dollars," he answers.

In my pocket, I have four green twenty-dollar notes. I can order two murders.

This is crazy. It has nothing to do with politics. Yet, during most of the Cold War, "experts" in the West tried to link drug trafficking with the East-West conflict. For example, the U.S. ambassador to Colombia from 1983 to 1985, Lewis Tambs, coined the term "narco-guerrilla" to describe guerrilla forces in remote regions of Colombia who work in partnership with cocaine producers. These guerrillas obviously exist, and they use violent tactics which can be described as terrorist. At the same time, they cooperate with the drug barons and are paid off not to interfere with narco-business. Therefore, they are very much part of the "aggression" against the United States.

"Partisans" are usually thought of in Latin America as armed troops connected organizationally or ideologically with leftist forces. There is the clear implication that drug "partisans" are tied to Communists and, in one way or another, to Moscow or Havana. This effort to associate communism with support of the drug trade has taken much more direct form. For example, take the following quote from Brian Crozier and Michael Seldon's 1986 book, *Socialism: The Grand Illusion:*

> The first to understand the power of drugs were the Chinese. Starting with the war in Korea, they distributed drugs among American GIs. After the Chinese, the Russians looked to drugs—they began to sell them to get hard currency, to corrupt the American army; they even tempted schoolchildren . . . of course the goal of the drug war by the Russians was the collapse of Western democracy.

Funny? To me, yes. But many other "respected" works such as this were published in the West. In *The Underground Empire: Where Crime and Governments Embrace,* James Mills wrote in 1986 of a hidden cocaine lab in the Colombian countryside guarded by helicopters and a military unit of FARC

(Revolutionary Armed Forces of Colombia), partisans directly connected to the Communists. Further, he said that FARC got aid from Cuba, and that FARC and another partisan group, the M-19, openly declared in the press that they were collecting tribute from drug traffickers . . .

The relations of partisan groups like FARC and M-19 with political parties were and are quite complex. I won't delve into them here, but I will say that by no means are all movements or partisan groups in Colombia leftist, and even less so are they all controlled by the Communists. M-19, for example, is more in tune with nationalistic forces in the bourgeoisie and intelligentsia than with leftists. But the idea dies hard that Communists are on the side of drug mafia and that, basically, it is leftists who are getting killed; if they are not Communists, then they are sympathizers.

As everyone knows, U.S.-Soviet relations have improved enormously since 1985. No longer are Soviets always the "bad guys" and Americans forever "good guys." Many of the old accusations have been relegated to the junk heap of history. In any case, there now exists the opportunity for the Soviet Union and the United States to work cooperatively to help stamp out the drug trade and narco-terrorism.

In 1989, the first steps were taken by the two governments to begin collaboration, and our U.S.-Soviet Working Group to Prevent Terrorism made initial recommendations on how the United States and the USSR can collaborate. In my view, these recommendations represent a good starting point for Soviets and Americans. Obviously, they do not speak to the root causes of drug traffic and narco-terrorism, but at least they provide a basis for our two countries to take common action. The recommendations include:

1. Providing mutual diplomatic support to governments currently attempting to combat the drug traffic.
2. Following the French government's proposals to attack "narco-money" and cooperating in joint efforts to restrict the laundering of funds derived from the drug traffic.
3. Developing economic and financial models to better un-

derstand the flow of drugs and money derived from the drug traffic.

4. Exchanging information on the production, smuggling, and distribution of narcotics, particularly in Southeast and Southwest Asia and Latin America, in accordance with existing agreements.
5. Sharing technology and expertise on methods to interdict illegal drug traffic.
6. Conducting further systematic studies of the phenomenon of narco-terrorism.
7. Exploring together the material and technical assistance requirements of countries that are on the front line in combatting drug production, in particular, Peru and Colombia.
8. Exploring alternate ways to reduce the consumption of drugs and the violence that accompanies the drug traffic.

CAMBRIDGE, MASS.: SEPTEMBER 1990

I looked again through all these points of Soviet-American cooperation. Yes, we have passed not a short distance within only one year of working together, crushing stereotypes from four decades of Cold War. We managed to channel our efforts against real evil, not one born in the heat of political debates.

This month, Harvard University presented the Louis Lyons Award for Conscience and Integrity in Journalism to Colombian journalists alive and dead who worked for El Espectador, *a Bogotá daily. The award received was by Luis Gabriel Cano, the man who took the place and obligations of Guilliermo Cano Isas, killed by narco-terrorists.*

I was at his funeral, a solemn and sad event. I could not help but think that if we Soviets and Americans had not lost forty-five years on the Cold War, not only his life but thousands of other lives might have been saved.

So simple and naive an idea, is it not?

CHAPTER 6

Emerging Techno-Terrorism

ROBERT KUPPERMAN

O nly a short time ago, we thought of terrorists as the disaffected children of European bourgeois societies, as the displaced refugees of the Middle East, or as people whose economic and social frustrations had erupted into violence. With that understanding, we comforted ourselves with the hope that these grievances could be addressed by social remedies.

Today's terrorist activities, however, have more to do with the realities of international conflict than with legitimate grievances. The ability of small nations to attack large ones, using the tactics of terror, has become painfully obvious. This brand of threat is so effective that it is becoming a political instrument of choice for nations such as Iran, Libya, and Syria. Terrorism has become warfare on the cheap. As a result, today's terrorist, rather than a bomb-throwing amateur, tends

Dr. Robert Kupperman is Senior Advisor at the Center for Strategic and International Studies and co-author of *Terrorism: Threat, Reality, Response.*

to be a professional, often trained by states, and well able to exploit a variety of modern technologies.

The highly technological thrust of contemporary terrorism is becoming its most worrying aspect. With the national intelligence services of hostile nations providing the wherewithal, planning assistance, and weapons, it is less clear what the political or technological limitations of terrorists will be. Terrorists now employ sophisticated encrypted communications systems once found only in arsenals of the great powers, as well as the range of sophisticated weapons and explosives usually associated with a modern army. Even more alarming is the spread of techniques for making radiological, chemical, and biological weapons. As these techniques filter into low-itensity conflicts—e.g., the use of chemical weapons in the Iran-Iraq war—the possibility for terrorist use increases in like measure.

Essentially, we see two primary areas of concern for future techno-terrorism: the use of relatively low-technology weapons against highly sophisticated targets; and the use of sophisticated means, including weapons of mass destruction, against key population targets. We will deal with each of these possible mutations of terrorism and then turn to the question of using technology as a first line of prevention and defense against techno-terror.

For the most part, terrorists have stuck to tried and tested patterns of attack—kidnappings, bombings, and hijackings. But their weapons and tactics have been substantially upgraded—trading in pistols for automatic weapons and pipe bombs for more efficient explosives. The hijack of a Kuwaiti airliner in 1988 by Shi'ite terrorists provides an illustrative case. In that episode, the terrorist team included at least one veteran of a previous hijacking as well as a pilot qualified to fly the aircraft. From the outset, the hijackers blocked the entry points on the plane by wiring the 747 with explosives. Careful planning, command, control, and communications rendered the jet virtually impervious to rescue. Similarly, the bombing of Pan Am 103 over Lockerbie, Scotland, later that year illustrated an upgrade of technological expertise. The bomb was preset with a multiphase trigger that sensed barometric pressure, takeoff and landing cycles, as well as measuring time.

The danger exists that terrorists will turn these improved capabilities against more critical, vulnerable targets. If technical expertise has grown, so too has the terrorist's ability to analyze and assess more sophisticated opportunities for attack. Attacks on civilian aircraft, while creating hundreds of individual tragedies, are largely containable. A particularly worrying terrorist mutation portends attacks on the lynchpins of a modern society; its technological infrastructure, including electric power, telecommunications and computer networks, oil and gas systems, transportation, and drinking water.

The horrifying prospect of such infrastructural attacks causes many officials simply to throw up their hands. The technological interconnections upon which we depend have become such an integral part of our lives as to be virtually invisible. Accidents within the infrastructure—the chemical accident at Bhopal; the oil spill from the *Exxon Valdez;* the radiological damage from Chernobyl—make the potential implications of deliberate sabotage grimly real. More deliberately targeted attacks could bring an industrialized society to a grinding halt through cascading disruption of interlocking networks.

Unfortunately, the potential for attacks on infrastructural targets is not a matter for speculation. Electric power facilities have been a magnet for terrorists for more than a decade in countries ranging from France to the Philippines, from the United States to Chile. Electric power facilities, precisely because they are a system upon which most other services depend, have become a target of choice. Damage control options become difficult once a complex, brittle electric grid has been taken off line. The problem extends beyond light and heat. In the most extreme case, a major and lengthy power failure could paralyze computer networks, food supply chains, sanitation and water systems, fuel, and transportation.

A few terrorist groups have made attacks on the infrastructure a particular specialty. The Shining Path in Peru has managed to black out the capital, Lima, on several occasions.

In 1984, the group blew up a strategic railroad bridge east of Lima which cut off food and mineral shipments. In Japan in 1978, the Khukaku-aha (or Middle Core) cut the cables leading to the control tower at Tokyo International Airport, forcing a halt in airport activity. In 1985, the group launched a much more sophisticated attack. Acting with military precision, helmeted terrorists simultaneously attacked thirty-four nodes of the national railway system, shutting it down and idling 18 million commuters. The group systematically sought and destroyed the electronic signalling cable that ran alongside the tracks. According to press reports, they then tried to increase panic by jamming police communications.

Attacks against the nuclear power electric industry offer potentially even more catastrophic implications. Certainly, nuclear reactors and violence are no strangers. Over the past 20 years, some 155 bombings and other attacks have taken place at the sites of civil nuclear installations in Sweden, Spain, the United Kingdom, France, Italy, Belgium, and the United States.

The danger is that a powerful bomb, such as the kind that killed 241 Marines in Lebanon in 1983, could conceivably crack the outer shell of a nuclear plant, leading to the release of radiation. Indeed, the Sandia National Laboratory has concluded that unacceptable damage to vital reactor systems could occur, not only from a relatively small explosive charge at close distances, but also from larger-size charges at distances greater than the protected area of some plants.

For the future, we must be concerned that new applications of technology will open up new avenues of attack. Computer software, for example, is extremely vulnerable to attack through computer viruses that can alter records, destroy data, or control systems. Such "viruses" are actually lines of code hidden within normal programming instructions. Like its biological counterpart, a computer virus has the capability to clone itself instantaneously and spread to every other computer program with which it comes into contact. A single strategically placed virus will rapidly infect thousands of other computers.

Viruses can be programmed to act immediately or to lie in wait for a predetermined trigger. A typical attack takes only hours to spread throughout a network. In biological terms, a computer virus is a disease that is infectious, spreads rapidly at the moment of contact, and may have no detectable symptoms until the moment it strikes. It also has no reliable "vaccine."

The existence of such viruses no longer belongs in the realm of science fiction. Computer viruses have been discovered in personal computer programs at corporations such as IBM, Hewlett-Packard, and Apple, and at major university centers, in Israel, West Germany, Britain, Italy, and the United States. "Friday the 13th" is the day often chosen for them to strike.

In 1988, an insidious attack with a computer virus was accidentally discovered in Israel. Designed as a weapon of political protest, the virus code contained a "time bomb" that would have caused all infected programs to erase their files on May 13, the fortieth anniversary of the demise of Palestine. The virus was discovered because of an error in its program which did not allow it to distinguish between uninfected and already infected programs. Because it continued to add copies of itself to infected software, in some cases up to 2,300 times, the extra lines of software began to flood disk memories, making the inserted lines of code easier to spot.

Later that year, a young U.S. computer whiz created a virus that disrupted operations in an estimated six thousand computers nationwide over a twenty-four-hour period. The student found a back door into a data network linking universities, defense contractors, and private research companies. His virus was programmed only to consume unused memory banks—although it could have been programmed to destroy existing ones—but a design error caused it to replicate widely, ultimately jamming all of the computers it infected.

What began as a student prank led to the most intensive scrutiny of the virus threat. Experts claim that it is difficult enough to identify random "bugs" in any computer program and virtually impossible to spot any deliberately inserted lines of code. But the possibility of terrorist use of computer viruses—potentially disrupting normal channels of international communications—gives rise to some disturbing questions about the future of techno-terror and its implications for national and international security.

Speculation about whether terrorists may use techniques of mass destruction will continue up to the day that an attack of such magnitude occurs. We will never resolve the hypothetical question with assurance one way or the other. What we can say is that the ability to execute a massively disruptive attack has increased through the proliferation of radiological, chemical, and biological resources and know-how.

The political barriers to such attacks are also eroding. In the past, it seemed reasonable to suppose, even if the technical barriers were surmounted, that terrorist groups would be refused safe haven if they went too far. No state would be willing to associate itself with madmen or risk retaliation for harboring terrorists who had crossed that tacit line of no return. Moreover, many presumed that as long as terrorists maintained an aura of social revolution, any action which threatened the lives of thousands of innocent people would have been difficult to defend.

As a form of interstate warfare, however, any presumption of rationality about terrorist acts has become less compelling. Since nations have begun to sponsor these events, the problems of safe haven are less critical. The pretext of social justice, too, appears threadbare when Syrian-backed suicide bombers attack American installations or Iranian-backed terrorists blow a Pam Am jumbo jet out of the sky. The bottom line is that it has become far less clear who will do what to whom and with what effect.

The fear of nuclear terrorism has run in tandem with concerns about nuclear proliferation. Unfortunately, the ability to design an atomic weapon is not as difficult as we once assumed. Indeed, a U.S. task force on nuclear terrorism concluded in 1987 that building a crude nuclear device, although difficult, is well within the reach of any terrorist group that can recruit three to four specialists.

While hardly an everyday occurrence, there have been a number of incidents of nuclear terrorism. Evidence surfaced in 1984 that linked the PLO with an Iraqi effort to purchase three atomic bombs. In 1985, a previously unknown American group sent letters to Turkish newspapers threatening to destroy three major Turkish cities with small nuclear devices. In the United States, there have been tens of nuclear weapons threats, although almost all have been fairly obvious hoaxes.

The problems associated with building a nuclear device nevertheless remain great. It is likely that only the most sophisticated, well-financed, and determined terrorist group would be able to surmount the hurdles involved in acquiring the fissile material, components, and expertise to construct and handle a nuclear device.

By contrast, the problems associated with simply dispersing radiological materials are trivial. Such substances—including iodine-131, plutonium-239, cobalt-60, cesium-137, and polonium-210—are found in hospitals and industrial facilities across the industrialized world and in largely unprotected pools of radiological waste around the globe.

The immediate shock value of radiological attacks—as measured in instant fatalities—is probably limited, given that it requires many years for their efforts to mature. As a weapon of horror, the threat to disperse radiological materials can be quite potent. In 1986, a threat to contaminate water reservoirs in New York City frightened many responsible officials. The threat was considered to be serious because the perpetrators clearly knew enough to choose a salt soluble in water.

Moreover, radiological agents could be a potent terrorist weapon for area denial, given that their half-lives are comparatively long. Suppose that a terrorist group were able to spread cobalt-60 in the World Trade Center in New York, Harrods department store in London, or any other public area in a major capital city. Vital commercial or financial centers could be forced to shut for months, even years. Rehabilitation would depend on whether the building could be cleared of hazardous materials and whether officials could justify the statistical risks of any long-term lingering physical threats.

These types of nuclear and radiological threats have been explored at length over many years and remain largely in the realm of the hypothetical. A concern of more recent vintage—also hypothetical—is that terrorists may turn to biological or chemical weapons to extend their mass destruction capabilities.

Chemical attacks will no doubt be facilitated by the proliferation of chemical weapon arsenals around the globe. Western intelligence services estimate that between fifteen and thirty countries now have, or are actively working to possess, chemical munitions. Also, the sheer availability of the ingredients for chemical weapons makes them a weapon of opportunity. The internationalization of the chemical industry—petrochemicals, fertilizers, and insecticides—has put the capability within reach of Third World countries and terrorist groups and virtually out of reach of any meaningful controls.

The widespread belief in a taboo against the use of such weaponry, particularly an apparent post-1918 consensus, is largely misplaced. In reality, chemical warfare has a long, infamous history. The ink was barely dry on the 1925 Geneva protocol banning chemical warfare when Spain dropped chemical bombs on Morocco. Italy sprayed toxic mustard gas during its conquest of Ethiopia, while Japan launched more than eight hundred gas attacks in Manchuria. The extensive use of chemical agents by Egypt during the Yemeni civil war in the sixties was followed by other incidents in the Persian Gulf, Afghanistan, and Nicaragua.

With the apparent loss of most lingering ethical or political restraints, the fabrication of chemical munitions is a relatively trivial task. There are literally tens of thousands of highly poisonous chemicals available for use. Among the most toxic are the organophosphous compounds—the so-called nerve agents—which have been described as "doing to humans what insect sprays do to bugs."

Terrorists have long had more than a passing interest in the extortion potential of chemical warfare. In recent years, Israeli security agents and police found cannisters of a potent poison, presumed to have been brought in by terrorists, at a safe house in Tel Aviv. In 1975, German entrepreneurs were apprehended in Vienna attempting to sell nerve agents to

Palestinian terrorists. Approximately 400 kilograms of intermediate compounds for the manufacture of nerve agents were discovered in a terrorist safe house in West Germany in the late seventies.

A far more lethal alternative are toxins, the poisonous byproducts of microorganisms, plants, or animals. Probably the best known toxin is botulism, with a virulence a thousand times more lethal than nerve agents. In a raid on a Red Army Faction safe house in 1980, French police found flasks of the unpurified toxin stored in the bathtub.

Another potent plant toxin is Ricin, a poison extracted from the castor bean. The most well publicized cases of Ricin poisoning occurred in 1978 against a pair of Bulgarian exiles. It is believed that each was attacked by means of an umbrella with an ingenious spring device that fired tiny steel pellets (the size of a pinhead) etched with microscopic grooves laced with Ricin. Such a pellet was found lodged in the back of one of the men and surgically removed just in time to save his life.

More ominous still is the as yet untapped potential for biological weapons. Pentagon officials claim that ten nations have developed a biological capability or are mustering the scientific know-how to genetically engineer new substances, including Iraq, Egypt, Iran, Israel, and Syria. There is little question that a determined state can put together the requisite components of a biological weapon without great difficulty. As expertise proliferates, however, it is quite possible that a trained technician could manufacture biological agents in a basement laboratory of only moderate sophistication. This might well put the capability in the hands of terrorist groups as well.

Traditionally, biological agents have not been a weapon of choice for a variety of reasons: prohibitive cost and the high risk of infecting friends as well as enemies. Today, dramatic advancements in the field of bio-technologies have changed the picture on bio-warfare. It is now theoretically possible to synthesize biological agents tailored to specifications: fast-acting incapacitants developed to fit climatic conditions or circumvent antidotes that the other side is suspected to possess.

New technology can also yield weapons against which the attacker can immunize himself in advance.

The ease of obtaining biological seedstocks was demonstrated in 1984 when two Canadians posing as microbiologists from the Canadian firm ICM Science ordered pathogens over the telephone from the American Type Culture Collection of Rockville, Maryland. When ATCC routinely sent a copy of the sales invoice to ICM Science, the large quantity of tetanus caught their attention. ICM Science recognized that it had not ordered the cultures and had no employees by the names given.

ATCC was in the news again in 1989 when Senator John McCain alleged that cultures of the tularemia bacteria had been shipped to Iraq from the Rockville Laboratory. It is widely assumed that Iraq will incorporate the bacteria stock—many times more infectious than anthrax—into its emerging biological weapons arsenal.

Terrorists and dissident groups have evinced a passing interest in biological weapons, although actual threats have been extremely limited. In the early seventies, the U.S. Army was reported to have been alerted to a plot by the Weathermen to steal a biological weapon from a fort in Maryland in order to poison the water supply of a major city. About that time, two American teenagers were charged with conspiracy to commit murder by introducing typhoid and other biological bacteria into the Chicago water supply.

What makes the prospect of biological weapons so nightmarish is the catastrophic power of even modest attacks, particularly in comparison to other superviolent weapons. For nuclear threats with a small subkiloton device, the fatalities in a major urban center could be in the order of several hundred thousand. A chemical attack with the most toxic substance available would probably not exceed a few thousand fatalities. But, for biological weapons, the numbers could theoretically run into millions, making biological attacks one of the most seriously frightening possibilities the world may face.

We should expect that terrorist attacks will grow more lethal for several reasons. First, the terrorists themselves are becoming more technologically adept, as demonstrated by the bomb that devastated the Marine barracks in Lebanon—among the largest non-nuclear blasts ever seen by U.S. experts—and the multiphase barometric triggering device used for devastating Pan Am Flight 103 on December 21, 1988. Second, governments willing to sponsor terrorism are providing the wherewithal—intelligence, logistical support, weapons—for attacks against new and more sophisticated targets. Third, religious and other radicals are establishing new boundaries for mass violence beyond what had been previously anticipated. Finally, the threshold for new forms of attack has already been breached. Attacks on the technological infrastructure, poisonings of municipal water supplies or medicinal stocks, thefts of radiological materials, while not all of terrorist origin, have created a clear precedent for future operations.

An effective defense against terrorism must be multilayered, including international cooperation, intelligence sharing, emergency preparedness, and effective law enforcement. In each of these areas, however, technology can offer invaluable new tools and techniques for counter-terrorism.

Indeed, there is a pressing need to bolster our technological capabilities against techno-terror. The objective is to raise the price of a terrorist attack, to lower the terrorist's probability of success, or to reduce the amount of real and perceived damage of a successful attack.

Although terrorists are becoming more technologically sophisticated, so too are the potential counter-terrorism applications. Technology plays a vital role in hardening targets, in facilitating cooperation through information sharing, and in managing terrorist incidents successfully. From remote sensing devices to rapid-entry techniques to computer-assisted conferencing, technology offers innovative offensive and defensive approaches.

For the spectrum of current threats, much more can be done in acquiring and implementing low-level technologies. One of the primary obstacles is in attitudes: we often act as though there is little more to be done to anticipate routine terrorist threats when, in fact, nothing could be further from the truth.

In airport security, for example, there exists an array of low-technology approaches which are not being systematically applied, including the widespread use of behavioral profiles, centralized intelligence and communications for all airlines, or better screening and training for security personnel. While we wait for better technologies to scan passengers' baggage, such as thermal neutron activation, we ought to be able to employ on-the-shelf options: low-pressure chambers which increase the relative vapor pressure of cached explosives so they can be sniffed more easily by dogs; or microwave chambers or sonic devices intended to resonate molecules in the explosive or electro-magnetic pulse (EMP) devices to detonate bombs in luggage.

Similarly, there is a range of potential counter-terrorism applications for high technologies on the shelf or on the horizon. Solid state cameras, smaller than an American 25-cent coin, can be hidden on aircraft to monitor hijackings in progress. Long-range infra-red devices which detect motion or the placement of individuals inside a hostage barricade are also available. Fiber optics—tiny hairlike strands of glass with a lens cover—can generate television pictures on the inside of a hostage operation.

Laser technologies, too, offer a host of new options against terror. Using lasers aimed through the windows of an aircraft or the glass panes of a building onto such items as a piece of paper, one might actually listen in on conversations inside a hostage area. Lasers might also be used as a means of communication to individual hostages by modulating minute concentrations of vapor. Though difficult to accomplish clandestinely, it is theoretically possible to communicate instructions to an individual hostage, e.g., to move a foot to the right to allow rescurers a clear shot.

Other devices include specialized explosives, high-powered sonic laser devices to disintegrate brick and mortar for rapid entry. Related techniques have been used for anti-personal objectives—to create temporary confusion or loss of body controls.

Information technologies can also play an important role in improving both emergency preparedness and the ability to cope effectively during a crisis. Modern digital equipment for more reliable communications, computer conferencing capabilities to allow multiple inputs across geographic distances, and the interactive use of computers for problem analysis are all available but largely unexploited technologies for domestic or international crisis management.

Although the emergency technology arsenal provides some extraordinary capabilities, a great deal more research and development must be done. The priorities can be grouped into four categories: current levels of threat; threats to the technological infrastructure; low probability/high consequences threat; and threat anticipation.

Current threats include bombings, hijackings, hostage taking, and their variants. Technology can assist in three key areas: intelligence and surveillance, protection and safeguards, and incident response.

Intelligence and surveillance, provided by a combination of traditional police methods and sophisticated technical systems, tend to be well supported because of the overlap with the needs of private business. For the most part, in this area, systems and services needed to deal with terrorism overlap with those needed for coping with other criminal threats.

Today, instead of a lone plant guard walking his beat, there are increasingly eleborate systems of electronic checks, door controls, monitors, sensors, automatic telephone call systems, and computer programs that help the user make rapid crisis assessments. A huge security industry, which some experts predict will reach $50–60 billion annually by the turn of the century, is devoted to access control and crisis prevention.

Nevertheless, it is not clear, particularly as terrorists grow more sophisticated, that counter-terrorism can be regarded as a small subset of a larger security problem. The types of defenses to thwart criminals and terrorists may not be identical, particularly in the event of massively disruptive attacks. More focused research for systems specifically applicable to terrorism defenses is still lacking.

Protection and safeguard technologies are today generally limited to barriers and various entry screening devices. Metal detectors, while useful in locating small arms, have fairly obvious weaknesses, notably their lack of utility in detecting non-metal firearms or high explosives in airline baggage. There are some new approaches, particularly in high explosives detection, under consideration. One of the most promising is neutron activation, a technique employed by the Israelis.

Response capability technologies can offer useful complements to conventional military or police methods. The near-term options under consideration include explosive disabling devices—firing a slug of ultra-cold material into an explosive to freeze its fusing mechanism; another is liquid metal embrittlement—weakening aluminum and magnesium metals to substantially reduce the amount of explosives needed to force entry through an aircraft door. The longer-term technological wish list might include more precise remote sensing devices to distinguish terrorists from their victims, low-profile anti-vehicle perimeters that shut down an internal combustion engine automatically, perhaps even techniques that can selectively impair brain functions or send commands (e.g., to put down the gun) directly to the brain.

In this area, the lack of understanding about where key nodes of vulnerability lie and how to defend them is the primary research gap. Private sector businesses are primarily concerned with their own tiny pieces of infrastructure, not with the integrity of the system as a whole. The technical characteristics and interconnections among various systems are so complex as to require highly sophisticated computer modeling and analysis, which can only be provided at the national or international level.

The scope for Soviet-American cooperation in this area is enormous. Joint efforts are required to prevent terrorists acquiring weapons and other equipment, especially weapons of mass destruction. Anti-terrorist technology should also be exchanged, consistent with the interests of each nation, nationally defined. The basic question is how much attention and funding we are prepared to devote to the offchance that we may be the victims of a highly destructive attack. In the United States, speculation about the threat of nuclear terrorism or the possibility of nuclear accidents led to the formation of the federal Nuclear Emergency Search Teams (NEST). NEST provides a rapid response capability, scientific knowledge and experience, a logistics and communications base, and specialized equipment in the event of a nuclear emergency. Unfortunately, no similar capability exists to respond to chemical, biological, or toxicological threats. One of the primary obstacles as well as an area of needed research is instrumentation to detect and identify such agents. While some chemical agent detectors and alarm systems are available off the shelf, detectors for biological or toxicological agents are not readily available. This is particularly true for long-range detection. By the time we can discern an aerosol cloud approaching, it is far too late to prevent a crisis. The Los Alamos National Laboratory has developed lasers to selectively excite aerosols of organic poisons, toxins, and live biologicals, but their value rests primarily in a military battlefield setting rather than in protection of civilian lives. Effective technologies for neutralization, immunization, and detoxification are either rudimentary or nonexistent.

Finally, research is needed to attempt to identify future threats and possible areas of research and development for response. Already, we can anticipate some of the countermeasures that may be needed in the future. We know, for example, that terrorists have downlink satellite receivers so that they can monitor cable news and network reports about their operation and potential counter-measures. We know too that they have experimented with portable uplink satellite transmitters to broadcast internationally—in effect, creating their own terrorism show. Any government wishing to avert humiliation and defeat ought to be preparing now to have the capability to selectively block transmissions in or out of a hijacked plane, train, or ship.

In many other areas, contingencies can be studied and responses prepared both at national and bilateral levels to turn the tables on terrorist operations and retain the offensive. Ultimately technology can offer no long-term solution to the problem of terrorism. What it can provide, however, is a new roster of capabilities to help prevent the terrorists from achieving their goals. New ways to assess our internal vulnerability, new physical safeguards against attack, and a more flexible and cutting edge technological advantage may create a truly credible deterrent against many attacks—especially those sponsored by states acting against common security interests of the United States and the USSR.

CHAPTER 7

U.S.-Soviet Cooperation—Requirements, Impediments, Context, and Implications

GLEB STAROUSHENKO AND MICHAEL STOHL

Ideally, bilateral cooperation between the United States and the Soviet Union, directed at the problem of terrorism, should be wide-ranging in its intent and prepared to address all aspects of the terrorist problem. Such an effort, however, is necessarily complicated by a need to preserve the two relatively distinct, often competitive and antagonistic, national security interests that are at the core of the political differences that have underlain the bilateral relationship of the superpowers for most of this century.

Terrorism, at first sight, seems an excellent candidate to begin cooperative problem solving. When identified as such, terrorism is unanimously condemned by political actors of all shades and backgrounds. Few in the contemporary world are

Gleb Staroushenko is Corresponding Member of the Soviet Academy of Sciences and Deputy Director of the Africa Institute.

Michael Stohl is Professor of Political Science and Associate Director of International Programs, Purdue University, editor of *The Politics of Terrorism,* and co-editor of *Current Perspectives on International Terrorism.*

ready to accept the designation "terrorist." Yet terrorism persists, provoking loud and frightened responses. This is out of proportion to the actual number of deaths. For terrorists in no way compare to the everyday horrors of malnutrition and preventable disease. Nor are the figures comparable to the deaths which result from regional conflicts and civil wars. The number of people who have lost their lives from acts of international terrorism in the past two decades is far exceeded by the number of victims of automobile crashes in the United States alone every year. This peculiar situation, where the social response to terrorism far exceeds the real scale of its currently existing reality, gives a clue to the utility of terrorism to its practitioners.

Contemporary terrorism gets its enormous impact from the internationalization of political processes and problems. These, which in the past were purely internal, have now gone beyond national boundaries. They have gone into the international sphere where there has been unprecedented development of economic, cultural, informational, and other connections between nations and states which have been sharply accelerated in our time by the development of the means of communication and transportation. In this situation many internal problems of countries have quickly acquired international repercussions, and they have become factors in affecting the international situation. It is not surprising that this new situation has led to a sharp enlargement of the international "stage" for the "theatrical presentations" for which many political extremists have such a weakness.

Terrorist actions are now calculated to create a maximum international response. These actions emphasize outrages designed to have a broad exposure in the world media—hijacking of airplanes on international flights; taking of foreign diplomats and soldiers as hostage; capturing embassies or consulates; attempts to kill people who have international reputations. The primary aim is not the concrete results of the "operations" but the public resonance: by taking aim at one person, one aims at thousands and even millions. In this sense, even force, which is the primary facet of terrorism, is not the goal of terrorism but a means—a megaphone with the aid of which the terrorists attract public attention, by their declared demands and programs as well as by their very existence. The mass media of information, with their desire for sensations and their taste for "action," are obediently carrying out the role that the terrorists have assigned to them—that of a loud-speaker or a sounding board which amplifies the echoes of their shots. Political dwarfs thus become Goliaths.

The operations of contemporary terrorists have begun to become refined as they have acquired real skill in being put on stage by the means of mass information. The press and television have been essential in starting criminal activities of terrorists because many of their actions wouldn't have been carried out at all if the organizers had not counted on a broad public seeing them. Certain operations of terrorists have been specially staged counting on the fact that they would be shown on television (e.g., the TWA hijack in Lebanon). Terrorists are extremely finely attuned to the important properties of the contemporary Western press with its chase for sensations, thrills, and so on. Announcements about the crimes of terrorists have been transformed by the Western media into supplements to the crime movies, a kind of new version of the horror movie, the only difference being that the average viewer has the thrill of knowing that it is not a matter of fake but real blood. At the same time, recourse by terrorists to the press is not a means of entering into some sort of public political discussion but rather a means of frightening the mass of people. It is just for this reason that the announcements are in the form of ultimata and make one think of the edicts of a military dictatorship, edicts that are posted in occupied populated places.

Why then has terrorism not previously been regarded by East and West as a common threat to their security? The main reason, of course, is that the post-1945 international system has been based on confrontation of antagonistic social systems on a world scale. The superpowers share mutual responsibility for this negative world political situation, which has become the soil for the growth of various kinds of terrorist groups identified with one side or other in the "Cold War."

The threat of destructive nuclear conflict between East and West sharply limited, and still limits, the possibility of open conflict between the military blocs in confrontation. This therefore set the stage for the operation of various unofficial groups. These have claimed to be able to solve the global conflicts at their level, sometimes operating independently, sometimes as the proxies of superpowers and other external forces. This kind of terrorism has emerged as a rule when we have dead-end situations in the international arena, when the normal mechanisms of political regulation of crises are no longer operating. It is in just such situations that the terrorists appear on the international scene, proposing their own simplistic solutions. Yet far from solving the problem of finding a more acceptable level of conflict, such terrorism raises the specter of another Sarajevo leading directly to a nuclear holocaust.

Until recently, the external politics of states with different social systems was based on the postulate that the conflict resulted from the presence between them of irreconcilable, antagonistic contradictions. The politics of each of the two basic military political blocs was based, if not on the destruction, then at least on the historical removal of the other social system from the international arena.

The reaction of the superpowers to the terrorist menace has reflected this mutual antagonism. Soviet analysts have largely ignored the problem of terrorism, simplifying it as a social evil inherent exclusively in "bourgeois, class antagonistic" society, directly attributable to the common crisis of capitalism and a consequence of the "aggressive external politics of the imperialist countries." In addition, attempts were made to legitimize the use of political force "for justified ends," to divide or to separate terroristic actions into "justified" and "non-justified," to confuse terrorism with national liberation struggles and assign to it in this way a kind of political alibi. Underlying these ideas was the shortsighted hope that terrorism as an external political phenomenon could be turned to do its deadly work exclusively in one direction—the direction of the

West. Western countries have also been guilty of a similar approach. They have arbitrarily separated the members of groups who used armed methods in a struggle into "terrorists" and "freedom fighters." The USA once even offered asylum to terrorists who had hijacked a Soviet airplane and killed a stewardess.

Such actions are now almost unthinkable. The growing interaction of the contemporary world means that political, economic, and social problems soon become common and global. This has been reflected in the phenomenon of terrorism. The Soviet Union and its allies have been inexorably drawn in. Some of their foreign representatives have been added to the list of terrorist victims. This contributed to the creation in Soviet eyes of an "objective base" for the creation of a world international cooperation in the struggle with this dangerous social phenomenon.

The Soviet Union now clearly expresses a new basic attitude toward terrorism as a criminal practice. In a 1989 statement concerning the murder of Lieutenant Colonel William Richard Higgins, the American UN military observer, the Soviet Union condemned terrorism in all its forms and manifestations as a blow to the rights of all mankind. There could be no justification, the Soviet Union said, for acts of terror such as kidnapping or reprisals against such acts. As *Pravda* made clear on August 4, 1989, the USSR supports "effective international measures aimed at preventing similar criminal acts and also for the immediate liberation of all hostages and kidnapped people held at the present time by whomsoever or wheresoever."

The United States has also tried to find a way out of the confusion between "terrorist" and "freedom fighter." George Bush, while still Vice President, proposed that we use international law. "The difference between terrorists and freedom fighters is sometimes not clear," he said in a foreword to a report in the Pentagon on terrorist groups published in 1989. "Speaking of one and the same person one could say he is a terrorist, others might say that he a freedom fighter." However, Bush says, terrorists are striving to destroy freedoms and democracy. They have selected as their goal civilians. "They are killing and maiming helpless men, women and children, their victims have become judges, journalists, legally elected official representatives, union leaders, and also policemen, priests and other people who believe in the values of a civilized society. Freedom fighters on the other hand are trying to maintain and adhere to international law and human rule and norms. The objects of their attacks are military goals and not unarmed civilians." Such analysis makes it possible to come to some generally shared conclusions about the content of the crime of terrorism and hence cooperation to deal with it.

Problem-solving approaches in any context must begin with such an assessment of the problem and an identification of the resources that may be brought to bear. They next define the conditions of trust that must be established within essentially adversarial relationships, and the benefits and costs of cooperative, non-cooperative, and antagonistic actions to the potential parties to the agreement. They must also then develop specific criteria which can be used to evaluate alternative solutions. K. J. Holsti, in *International Politics* (1988), argued that the conditions likely to "generate and support cooperation and policy coordination" among nations are similar or complementary state interests, purposes, and needs; equitable distribution costs of risks, burdens, and rewards; trust that commitments will be fulfilled; and interactions conducted on the basis of reciprocity, reliability, and predictability.

In short, the parties who are confronted by a "common problem" or those who propose to use their resources to address a situation which might have potential to become a common problem, need to establish to themselves that the "other" perceives the problem as serious and one that is amenable to attempted solutions. They further must believe that it is in their interest that the problem actually be solved. Thus, the parties must perceive that (a) from a positive viewpoint, there is benefit to be gained by solving the problem; and/or (b) from a negative viewpoint, there is no inherent advantage to them that the problem continue to be a problem because it hurts others more than it hurts them.

With particular respect to the United States and Soviet Union, Alexander George has argued in his recent study of *U.S.-Soviet Security Cooperation* (1988) that two factors are especially important in generating security cooperation. They are

> (1) the perception by a superpower that it is dependent to some extent on the other superpower's behavior to assure or improve some aspect of its overall security; and (2) the judgement that strictly unilateral measures, however important and necessary, will either not suffice to deal adequately with a particular threat to its security that the other side can pose or are too expensive or risky. When both sides experience these perceptions their awareness of mutual dependence on each other for security is accompanied by feelings of vulnerability. This in turn arouses incentives for exploring cooperative arrangements.

Within this context, "any particular cooperative agreement is judged to be acceptable or not depending on whether its expected results will indeed further the actor's security and foreign policy interests." In this, the logic mirrors the "realist" analysis that the principle which should underlie the forming of alliances is expediency. Agreements between friends and antagonists, if they are to be viable and durable, must be built upon an interest and a need to cooperate, not a perception that it would be "nice" if the antagonists would cooperate.

A problem such as terrorism, which threatens both superpowers, has multiple and complex sources and no singular solution. It requires the allocation of vast resources and threatens great costs should no solution be found. Since a solution to the problem would have tangible benefits, it provides an ideal, although complex and thorny, problem about which to cooperate. Thus, clear payoffs are available for the superpowers. In the grand strategic sense, we may suggest that by cooperating they can make international politics and the international system safe—or safer—for their competition and rivalry. Great powers have always sought mechanisms by which to regulate their environment and their rivalry so as to control the potential risks and the possible costs.

Having said this, there is no question that there are clear impediments to both general questions of cooperation between the United States and the Soviet Union and specific issues which may arise from the particular problems of terrorism. In his discussion of the requirements for building cooperation introduced above, Holsti makes it clear that these requirements are most likely to be fulfilled in situations in which the states that attempt cooperation are (1) not closely linked or intertwined, or (2) already define themselves as existing within a security community, or (3) are part of universal relationships that are linked to narrow technical or economic issues. Since the United States and the Soviet Union, by virtue of their position as superpowers, define themselves as intertwined globally, as adversaries not within the same security community, and as powers who prefer to solve their own problems, none of these conditions directly and easily may be applied to the U.S.-Soviet relationship and the problem of terrorism. Thus any agreement on terrorism by the superpowers, in the absence of a transformation of the basic situation and/or perceptions of the superpowers' adversaries, must occur in the context of continuing competition. Under such circumstance, as Alexander George argues, for a "cooperative agreement to be acceptable it must not be judged by either side as seriously handicapping it in the continuous competition."

The most serious impediments to cooperation on terrorism arise from the nature of the superpower relationship itself. This relationship creates fundamental difficulties which must be addressed within any attempt to create cooperative arrangements. It is interesting to note that this is not an area that U.S. analysts on Soviet-American relations have addressed. Even the most recent work continues to ignore the issue. For example, Miroslav Nincic, in *Anatomy of Hostility: The U.S.-Soviet Rivalry in Perspective,* an otherwise perceptive and informative analysis of U.S.-Soviet relationships, does not address the question of terrorism; nor do Alexander George and his colleagues Farley and Dallin in *U.S. Security Co-Opera-*

tion: Achievements, Failures, Lessons, despite the fact that their entire volume of high-quality essays is focused on the U.S.-Soviet "security" relationship.

However, there is general agreement among such writers that a set of structural disincentives to cooperation shapes current givens in the superpowers' formulation of their relationship. First, both the United States and the Soviet Union are unlikely to acknowledge signs of conciliatory intent on the part of the other. It takes much greater evidence of good behavior and benign intent on the part of an adversary than on the part of an ally to convince a skeptic that the behavior is intended as positive or is compliant. Second, it remains the fact that whenever and whatever cooperation unfolds, there is a deeply held belief on the part of each superpower that short of the collapse of the adversary there is no guarantee of the end to the adversarial relationship. In its more extreme forms this may be characterized as the "demonological" perspective, with all forms of trouble arising from or benefiting the adversary and hence reinforcing to the adversarial relationship. The result is an inherent momentum of continued hostility. The issues that create the superpower rivalry are fundamental, they are core values and strike at the heart of the state and national security. While the possibility of failure is equated with an end to civilization as we know it, i.e., the loss by one superpower to the other, the possibility of success is always only a finite increase in security.

The onus in security discussions therefore falls on those who push cooperative rather than unilateral solutions to demonstrate not merely that they might help but more importantly to guarantee that they will not harm. Given the context of suspicion and hostility, ambiguous evidence is more safely interpreted in negative terms. This is the case both for strategies in an international sense and for domestic politicians and interest groups who believe they benefit from the continued hostility and fear that the superpower adversarial relationship brings.

This is not to argue that advances in cooperation between the Soviet Union and the United States are not possible, but rather to recognize that there are fundamental impediments between adversaries that interfere with the already difficult problem of dealing with the threat of terrorism. When you trust your possible partner, you seek the things you may do together. When you don't trust him, you seek those things plus the assurance that he won't do all the possible things you could imagine to betray both the agreement and all those things you may have forgotten to explicitly address. Within such a context, it is imperative that any agreement or set of agreements in principle incorporate provisions that will convince skeptics that violations of the agreement have costs to the violator which at the least, if discovered, will greatly exceed the benefits of violation. This is the same principle as would be found in a secure, "verifiable" arms control agreement.

Finally, what are the implications of such cooperative enterprises for the basic superpower adversarial relationship, and more particularly the spillover to their formal allies in NATO and the Warsaw Pact and their informal network of supporters and dependent states and state challengers? As the record on reactions to arms control initiatives has shown, there is much nervousness even amongst the closest of allies about possible agreements, and even more in the mere improvement of relationships between the superpowers when their closest allies are not direct participants in the process. On this particular issue, Third World state challengers are most likely to be suspicious of being "sold out" for overarching superpower interests in reducing threats to themselves as opposed to supporting the goals of their movements. Further, domestic supporters of these state challengers within the superpowers themselves will also need political reassurance. Agreements by the superpowers on measures to reduce the risk of terrorism must not be presented as a means to end conflicts that divide states and peoples. Rather, they must be seen as a mechanism by which to create boundaries that place the use of terrorism outside "legitimate" political behaviors, regardless of the validity of the cause.

Such mechanisms should reduce the risk of terrorist events

escalating into superpower confrontations, reduce the likelihood and frequency of terrorist attacks in general and with the superpowers as the target in particular, reduce the magnitude, scope, and intensity of damage and casualties of terrorist attacks that do occur, and improve the capability of the superpowers to monitor, respond, and investigate terrorist events. They would include:

1. Creation of a standing bilateral group and channel of communications for exchange of information on terrorism—in effect, a designated link for conveying requests and relaying information during a terrorist crisis.
2. Provision of mutual assistance (information, diplomatic assistance, technical assistance, etc.) in the investigation of terrorist incidents.
3. Exchange of anti-terrorist technology, consistent with the national security interests as defined by each nation.
4. Prohibition of the sale or transfer of military explosives and certain classes of weapons (such as surface-to-air missiles) to non-government organizations, and increased controls on the sale or transfer to governments.
5. Initiation of bilateral discussions on requiring chemical or other types of "tags" in commercial and military explosives to make them more easily detectable and to aid in the investigation of terrorist bombings.
6. Initiation of joint efforts to prevent terrorists from acquiring chemical, biological, nuclear, or other means of mass destruction.
7. Conduct of joint exercises and simulations in order to develop further means of Soviet-American cooperation during terrorist threats or incidents.

The initial proposal, creation of a designated link, is on the surface the least complicated, least costly, and perhaps "safest" of the suggestions. It requires mainly goodwill and involves little in the way of the provision of organizational resources. There are no formal mechanisms attached in the description of how and where the designated link would be located in the respective governments, but it is hoped that negotiations between the two governments would find such a link at a level appropriately high enough that the superpowers would be assured of its performing the information distribution and risk reduction roles that are intended. This link might easily be connected with the mutual assistance and technology exchange functions of proposals 2 and 3, or it might simply be reserved for potential crisis management purposes. The advantages of such a link are in its potential for "routinization" of the exchange of information (chosen by the *provider*, not the *recipient*), and the low-risk, low potential cost of the link. Looking to the misuse of the link, what could be lost by a cooperative partner to misuse? The most likely "misuse" is actually "no use." That is, the most likely negative outcome is a decision by one superpower not to "answer" the link. There are no possible benefits to be gained that are inherent in its misuse. In the context of superpower blocs and formal allies and less formal support and dependency networks, some nations and groups may be uneasy about regularized channels between the superpowers, but this should not be a major diplomatic problem.

When we move from the general question of a designated link to the concepts implied by the exchange of information and technology in proposals 2 and 3, possible payoffs and problems begin to emerge. The adoption and working arrangements of these two proposals require an interest and willingness to allow each side to define, for itself, what it is willing to consider as appropriate information and technology to transfer. If governments are approaching these proposals from a stance that seeks to encourage the development of such exchanges, then the governments will have to understand the risks, costs, and benefits of a willingness to provide too much or too little, as well as the risks of indicating that one has little to provide or needs to request certain assistance.

There is further the risk that a government will seek to provide misleading, false, or useless information to gain a short-term advantage because it calculates that the loss of the long-term interest in cooperation is worth the risk. There is also the risk that governments will request information that they either know the other cannot provide because it is a political powder keg or cannot provide because it is incapable and hence its limitations may be exposed. It is important to understand that with much "intelligence" information, the mere provision of information can jeopardize the source and thus further access to important information. Therefore, it is always possible that one side in a cooperative arrangement, no matter how cooperative, will not reveal all. In the short run this will in the context of the adversarial arrangement breed distrust. Thus, multiple opportunities must be sought, and if possible useful information shared, if the proposal is to bear any fruit.

This analysis of the inherent perils of the exchange of intelligence information leads on to a suggestion that a sensible arrangement based on these proposals is one that is always posed in terms of a general request for assistance, and that is responded to at the time in a manner which is deemed acceptable by the provider and not the recipient. Recipient complaints will need to be made quietly (perhaps through the designated link); and such complaints only serve a purpose if they push toward an expansion of cooperation rather than simply announcements of shortcomings.

Proposals 4, 5, and 6 involve creating mechanisms and procedures for limiting the possible damage that terrorists may be able to do, and increasing the chance that if terrorists employ certain classes of weapons, they will be easier to detect and/or trace after the fact. These proposals are therefore more likely than the previous three proposals to require "upfront" discussions within the political and decision-making framework of each of the superpowers as to the clear political choices, costs, and implications that are involved, before the terrorist events take place.

Of the three, proposal 6, to prevent the acquisition of weapons of mass destruction by terrorists, is on the surface the most obvious of goals and the least objectionable. While neither superpower is likely to want to argue for the provision of such weapons to possible terrorists, nor actually to provide such weapons, a more important question concerns the transfer of raw materials. Such transfers make mass destruction weapons possible for states that are allied to the superpowers, and from whom terrorists may be enabled to obtain the materials or the knowledge necessary to construct certain classes of weapons. The logic of this proposal is the same underlying the Nuclear Non-Proliferation Treaty. However, that logic notwithstanding, there are nations that did not sign the treaty, and signatories who have complied with the letter of the law and cooperated with nations to acquire materials for the "peaceful" use of nuclear energy whose security arrangements would be judged less than adequate by many outside observers. Nonprovision of nuclear materials has caused strains between the superpowers and their dependents; it has also resulted in the provision of such materials because of future market possibilities and/or other long-term diplomatic or material concerns.

Proposal 4, prohibiting the transfer of certain classes of weaponry to insurgents and states, will involve a calculus by the superpowers that it is better to reduce the possibilities that those each side supports will have the finest military means at their disposal than to risk terrorists gaining weapons they can turn on the superpowers and their allies. It will require the balancing of short- and long-term interests and an analysis of the arms market to calculate if others will merely fill the void left by the superpowers. If the latter likelihood is strong, it will push the superpowers to expand the level of cooperation on this issue to the other potential suppliers, or will make it less likely they will be able to balance the calculations to a cooperative agreement.

The "tagging" of an explosive would enable investigators to locate the source of supply. If it comes from a superpower-controlled arsenal, it may prove to be very embarrassing and potentially escalatory, unless such a "batch" of explosives had been reported as stolen, missing, or whatever. This would push the superpowers to increase their recommended levels of security and monitoring of such security arrangements so as not only to reduce the risk of terrorists employing such materials, but also to reduce the risk that they will be connected, even if merely by negligence, to an event. This should have the net effect of dampening the available supply.

Such methods may also aid in the detection of the covert transportation of explosives by "tagging," which would be linked to the development of further detection devices. Consistent behavior on such mechanisms would enable the superpowers to push for the spread of technical explosives standards that would generate their own momentum, given the utility in countering the threat to other nations. Hence beyond the loss of certain specific patent opportunities there should be few long-term costs associated with such an approach.

The final proposal, the development of joint exercises and simulations, would provide an environment within which to learn how each side views terrorist events and risks, and how they attempt to manage events that occur and those that may threaten. Role-playing exercises serve to teach the participants how their superpower adversary interprets their actions and inaction. They demonstrate how seemingly straightforward pieces of information may be interpreted very differently, and how what may be perceived as positive actions or benign inaction may be misinterpreted as harmful or unhelpful.

Beyond the lessons that may be learned from the analysis of the interactions that all such simulations, games, and exercises should provide, the regularity of such games provides the opportunity for multiple participants and thereby the establishment of networks of "experts" concerned with the problem. They will have greater appreciation of the intentions, style, and constraints of their counterparts as they try jointly, within the overall adversarial relationship, to manage the threat that terrorists imply to both sides.

There are dangers in such exercises. They may help reveal significant gaps in knowledge and significant weaknesses in decision making. They may, on the other hand, make the other side feel that one set of decision makers has far more access to knowledge than it does, thus leading to suspicions beyond the game situation that there is an unwillingness to help rather than an inability. They may provide a false sense of decision-making superiority or inferiority. These dangers notwithstanding, a prudent selection of players, and a commitment to multiple efforts, should greatly improve each side's understanding of the interests of the other in reducing the threat of terrorism, and their respective abilities to assist the other. The danger of the Emperors wearing no clothes appears outweighed by the possibilities that they will provide each other with the skills and materials to make new ones.

Our analysis of the requirements, context, impediments, and implications of the seven bilateral measures proposed above indicates clearly that cooperation by the United States and the Soviet Union on the question of terrorism has much to recommend it, but also many sources of difficulty and many potential minefields. Generating the will to cooperate within an essentially adversarial relationship is not a simple matter, even if there are clear security gains that may be achieved. Sustaining the will and providing the rewards of cooperation while accepting the continuity of the adversarial relationship is even more difficult. In the self-help context in which nations find themselves within the international system, all cooperative enterprises will only be sustained if they provide gains without increased risks of loss. We believe that the seven suggestions, with the provisos indicated, provide a useful place from which to begin to test the utility of the growth of cooperative efforts to confront the problem of terrorism, while posing minimal risks to the basic security interests of the superpowers.

CHAPTER 8

Legal Dimensions of U.S.-Soviet Cooperation in Combatting Terrorism

JOHN F. MURPHY AND VALENTIN ROMANOV

Until recently, cooperation between the United States and the Soviet Union in combatting terrorism would have appeared, to most observers, at best a remote possibility. Far from cooperating to combat terrorism, the United States and the Soviet Union had traded charges that the other was actively engaged in sponsoring international terrorism. In 1981, for example, then U.S. Secretary of State Alexander Haig charged that the Soviet Union was seeking to "foster, support and expand" terrorist activities around the world and that it was "training, funding and equipping the forces of terrorism." Other U.S. observers made similar charges. For its part, the Soviet Union has claimed that the United States "is more and

John F. Murphy is a professor at Villanova University Law School; former Chairman of the American Bar Association's Committee on International Institutions Law; and author of *Punishing International Terrorists: The Legal Framework for Policy Initiatives* and *State Support of International Terrorism: Legal, Political, and Economic Dimensions.*

Valentin Romanov of the Institute of World Economy and International Relations, USSR Academy of Sciences, is a former Soviet ambassador.

more openly relying on force, interference in the affairs of free nations, and state terrorism."

During the 1970s, in particular, the United States and the Soviet Union were working at cross purposes. It will be remembered that the kidnapping and killing at Munich on September 6, 1972, of eleven Israeli Olympic competitors by Arab terrorists, as well as a number of other spectacular acts of terrorism, resulted in the UN General Assembly considering the problem of international terrorism and in the introduction by the United States on September 25 of a Draft Convention for the Prevention and Punishment of Certain Acts of International Terrorism. In introducing the convention, and in subsequent debates on it, U.S. representatives attempted to obviate the concern of some member states (including the Soviet Union) that the convention was directed against wars of national liberation. To this end, they pointed out that the convention was limited in its coverage to "any person who unlawfully kills, causes serious bodily harm or kidnaps another person . . . ," that the act had to be committed or take effect outside of the state against which the act was directed, unless such acts were knowingly directed against a non-national of that state, and that the act must not be committed either by or against a member of the armed forces of a state in the course of military hostilities. Despite these efforts, many member states opposed the U.S. initiative, viewing it as directed generally against revolutionary movements. As a result, the General Assembly adopted a resolution on measures to prevent international terrorism, by which an ad hoc committee was established to deal with the problem, but failed to take any action on the U.S. draft convention.

The Soviet Union, which, as the UN 1972 *Yearbook* put it, "also favored the conclusion of a convention," felt that it would be premature to consider convening an international conference on the subject. Instead, the USSR suggested that the UN International Law Commission be invited to prepare a draft as quickly as possible. A similar idea was embodied in the fourteen-power draft resolution co-sponsored, inter alia, by a number of Western countries, including Belgium, Canada,

Italy, and the United Kingdom. But the draft shared the fate of that tabled by the USA: it was not put to the vote. The General Assembly resolution referred to above was adopted on the basis of the sixteen-power draft submitted by non-aligned countries.

The lesson to be learned from this unfortunate development is clear: having found themselves divided on an issue which seemed to be of a more procedural than substantive nature (where to make the convention in question, at a conference or an International Law Commission session?), the United States and the USSR have failed to make progress on the much more important problem of substance. Almost twenty years have now elapsed from the early seventies, but the United Nations is still discussing the issue of concluding a convention to eradicate international terrorism.

However, for both the United States and the USSR it is not just a routine failure to take a common position on a procedural issue. The underlying cause of the disagreement runs much deeper: the Soviet Union has shared the apprehensions of Third World countries that certain actions by national liberation movements could be associated with acts of international terrorism. Already in 1973, in comments submitted to the Ad Hoc Committee on International Terrorism, the USSR expressly argued that prohibitions against—much less less criminal sanctions for—terrorist acts could not apply to wars of national liberation.

All this development was the low point for those who had hoped that the United States and the Soviet Union might cooperate in combatting terrorism. As we shall see later in this chapter, the United States and the Soviet Union have since managed to agree in various international forums on cooperative measures to combat international terrorism. Since the accession to power of President Mikhail S. Gorbachev, moreover, the Soviet Union has expressed an enhanced interest in combatting international terrorism irrespective of its motives, origin, and perpetrators. It also has been highly critical of specific terrorist acts. For example, in 1985 the Soviet Union characterized the U.S. reaction of outrage against the *Achille*

Lauro hijacking and the murder of passenger Leon Klingh-offer as "understandable and just," and called for severe pun-ishment of the terrorists, who were members of the Palestine Liberation Front. Similarly, in response to the September 1986 hijacking attempt by the Abu Nidal Organization against a U.S. airliner in Pakistan which resulted in twenty-one deaths, *Pravda* was sharply critical: "No matter what the mo-tives of the people who committed this evil deed, there is no justifying it. . . . A resolute stop must be put to terrorism of all sorts. . . . These criminal actions must not be allowed to end people's lives, jeopardize the normal course of international relations, severely exacerbate some situation, or engender vio-lence. . . ." Also condemned were the several bombings in Paris in the fall of 1986.

In the United Nations the USSR started promoting a com-prehensive approach to international security, which would include as its inherent component the unconditional elimina-tion of international terrorism and the establishment of a tribunal to prosecute its perpetrators. The Soviet Union and the United States have cooperated in several actions directed against international terrorism. These include, among others, the adoption, on December 9, 1985, of a General Assembly resolution that *"unequivocally condemns* as criminal, all acts, methods and practices of terrorism wherever and by whom-ever committed, including those which jeopardize friendly re-lations among States and their security"; the adoption on De-cember 18, 1985, of a Security Council resolution whereby the Council condemns *"unequivocally* all acts of hostage taking and abduction"; and the adoption, in July 1988, of a Security Council resolution which calls for the release of Lieutenant Colonel William Richard Higgins, who was a United Nations Truce Supervision Organization military observer serving with the United Nations Interim Force in Lebanon (UNIFIL) at the time of his abduction. The United States and the Soviet Union were co-sponsors of this resolution.

Most significantly, in December 1987, the Soviet Union and the United States joined in a successful effort aimed at prompting the UN membership to reach a consensus compromise decision when Syria tabled a proposal that would have had the United Nations convene an international conference to define the difference between terrorism and the legitimate right of oppressed peoples to fight for national freedoms. This was seen by many countries as an attempt to legitimize international terrorism if committed by a national liberation movement. A compromise resolution was adopted that reaffirmed the 1985 resolution of the General Assembly condemning terrorism.

At its forty-fourth session in the fall of 1989 the General Assembly requested the International Law Commission, a subsidiary organ of the Assembly, to address the question of establishing an international criminal court with "jurisdiction over persons alleged to have committed crimes which may be covered under a code, including persons engaged in illicit drug trafficking across national frontiers." The Assembly also decided to consider the question of establishing such an international criminal court at its forty-fifth session when examining the report of the International Law Commission. We believe that the United States and the Soviet Union should support the concept of an international criminal court, and we set forth some suggestions as to the form this support might take in the last section of this chapter.

The stage may now be set for enhanced U.S. and Soviet cooperation in combatting terrorism. If so, the strengthening of national and international law and institutions designed to combat terrorism will be an important part of this cooperation. Accordingly, this chapter turns first to a description and evaluation by the respective authors of U.S. and Soviet national law on international terrorism. Next it considers international law on terrorism, especially those treaties that the United States and the Soviet Union both have ratified. Then it evaluates existing institutional arrangements within the United Nations, its specialized agencies, and some other international institutions, such as the International Criminal Police Organization (INTERPOL). Lastly, the chapter sets forth conclusions and recommendations for change in national and international law, as well as proposals for new institutional arrangements to combat terrorism.

United States national law on international terrorism is vast and wide-ranging. A 1987 compilation of "Major Laws, Treaties, Agreements, and Executive Documents," drawn up by the Congressional Research Service, runs to 962 pages. Extensive discussions of this law are available elsewhere. Our effort here is to pinpoint salient aspects of U.S. law (other than international law) and to evaluate their usefulness in combatting international terrorism.

We limit our consideration to laws on terrorism relating to the following three areas: intelligence, substantive criminal law, and economic sanctions. Although a number of states in the United States (California, for example) have laws on terrorism, these are of relatively little interest from an international perspective.

Intelligence

There is general agreement that the collection and use of intelligence is an effective tool in combatting terrorism. Ideally, the gathering of intelligence serves a preventive role and enables law enforcement officials to intercept terrorists at an early stage, before they inflict injury on persons or property. This has proven, however, to be a difficult task.

During the 1970s in the United States, revelations of a history of executive abuse of the intelligence services for partisan political purposes convinced many, including Congress, that the intelligence community required stricter supervision. In particular the work of congressional investigatory committees highlighted the intrusive nature of electronic surveillance and led to the adoption of the Foreign Intelligence Surveillance Act (FISA). FISA contains the primary federal statutory definition of "international terrorism," which means activities that

(1) Involve violent acts or acts dangerous to human life that are a violation of the criminal laws of the United States or of any State, or that would be a criminal violation if committed within the jurisdiction of the United States or any State;

(2) Appear to be intended—
     (a) To intimidate or coerce a civilian population;
     (b) To influence the policy of a government by intimidation or coercion; or
     (c) To affect the conduct of a government by assassination or kidnapping; and

(3) Occur totally outside the United States, or transcend national boundaries in terms of the means by which they are accomplished, the persons they appear intended to coerce or intimidate, or the locale in which their perpetrators operate or seek asylum.

It is important to note that FISA's definition does not serve as the basis for imposition of criminal penalties, nor as the standard for economic sanctions against the countries that support international terrorism. Rather, it serves only as a predicate for application of the electronic surveillance permitted by the Act under certain circumstances.

FISA permits the collection of intelligence by electronic surveillance of persons in the United States participating in our preparing for international terrorist activities, but requires a judicial warrant for such surveillance with certain limited exceptions. It defined "foreign intelligence information" in part as "information that relates to, and if concerning a United States person, is necessary to, the ability of the United States to protect against . . . sabotage or international terrorism by a foreign power or an agent of a foreign power."

There are exceptions to the general requirement that a judicial warrant be obtained for all electronic surveillance for foreign intelligence purposes. The President, through the Attorney General, may authorize electronic surveillance for up to one year without a warrant if the Attorney General certifies under oath that the surveillance will be directed exclusively at communications between foreign powers. This surveillance must be conducted in such a way that there is no substantial likelihood that the communication intercepted will be one to which a U.S. citizen is a party, and it must be performed in accordance with procedures spelled out in the statute.

A second exception to the warrant requirement under the Act permits electronic surveillance under certain emergency circumstances, but a warrant must be obtained within twenty-four hours after the surveillance is conducted.

In the absence of one of the exceptions, a warrant must be obtained from one of seven district court judges specially designated by the Chief Justice of the United States to hear and approve applications for electronic surveillance anywhere in the United States. Appeal from denial of an application may be taken to a three-judge panel selected by the Chief Justice from the district courts or the courts of appeal.

Under FISA there are two types of court order, and hence two different forms of application, depending upon whether the target of the electronic surveillance is an "official" foreign power (i.e., a foreign government, a faction of a foreign nation, or an entity openly acknowledged by a foreign government to be controlled by that government) or not. For "non-official" foreign powers or agents (i.e., a group engaged in international terrorism, a foreign-based political organization, or an entity directed or controlled by a foreign government), each application for an order must include the name of the federal officer making the application; a statement showing that the President has delegated authority to the Attorney General to approve such applications and that the Attorney General did approve the application; the identity or a description of the target; and a statement of facts that support the applicant's affirmation that the target is a foreign power or an agent of a foreign power. The application must also set forth proposed "minimization" procedures, a detailed description of the nature of the information sought and the types of communications to be monitored. The Assistant to the President for National Security Affairs must certify that the information sought is foreign intelligence information within the meaning of the Act and is not obtainable by other means. Finally, the application must include the history, if any, of past applications for this same target, whether physical entry is necessary to accomplish the electronic surveillance, the types of surveillance devices to be used, the means by which they will be installed, and the period of time for which the surveillance is to be monitored.

If the order sought is for surveillance of an "official" foreign power, and if the premises to be subject to the surveillance are owned, leased, or exclusively used by one of these targets, less information is required to obtain a court order. Then there is no requirement that the application describe the nature of the communications sought, the type of communications to be monitored, the means by which the surveillance will be accomplished, or that it detail the types of surveillance devices to be employed.

In deciding whether to issue an order, a judge examines the application to determine whether there is probable cause to conclude that the target is a foreign power or an agent of a foreign power and that the facilities at which the surveillance is directed are or will be used by the target. If the target is a U.S. national, the judge must find that the certification by the Assistant to the President for National Security Affairs is not "clearly erroneous."

In most instances the judge's order approves electronic surveillance for ninety days, although a year is permitted if the target is an official foreign power. An extension may be granted on the same basis as the original order, except an extension for surveillance of non-official foreign powers may be for a year if probable cause is found to conclude that no communication of any U.S. person will be involved. The judge may assess compliance with the order at any time during the surveillance or at the end of the surveillance period.

With a few exceptions, FISA has been generally praised as permitting effective intelligence gathering while providing sufficient fourth amendment protections for prospective targets of electronic surveillance. It has been noted, however, that there are arguably two major gaps in coverage in the Act. It does not explicitly regulate foreign intelligence physical searches; and it does not cover searches or surveillance engaged in by U.S. intelligence agencies abroad.

Despite efforts to do so, FISA has not been amended to fill these gaps. Most important for present purposes, neither FISA nor any other U.S. legislation expressly regulates electronic surveillance abroad. Rather, constraints on electronic surveillance and other methods of intelligence gathering abroad have come from presidential executive orders, the latest of which is President Reagan's Executive Order 12333, congressional oversight based on such legislation as the Intelligence Oversight Act of 1980, and executive branch oversight through such mechanisms as the President's Foreign Intelligence Advisory Board and the President's Intelligence Oversight Board.

The debate between Congress and the executive branch over intelligence activities has centered primarily on two issues: control over covert actions; and the right of Congress to have access to sensitive intelligence information. With respect to the gathering of intelligence abroad, through electronic surveillance or other means, the executive branch has basically been given free rein. The legislative history of the National Intelligence Act of 1980, for example, reveals a willingness of Congress to allow the President to approve physical searches of U.S. citizens abroad if "extraordinary circumstances require such collection to acquire foreign intelligence that is essential to the national security of the United States and that cannot reasonably by acquired by other means."

If there are relatively few constraints on U.S. intelligence agencies with respect to the collection of intelligence, the situation is more problematical with respect to the availability and the dissemination of such information to government officials with primary responsibility for combatting terrorism. Similarly, there are concerns that such information, once collected and disseminated, may be subject to mandatory public disclosure.

Specifically, provisions of the Privacy Act of 1974 raise questions about the dissemination of information regarding terrorist activities to foreign governments. These provisions do not clearly preclude such dissemination, but contain certain ambiguities that render applicable limits uncertain. Although these ambiguities were identified over a decade ago, they remain unresolved.

Foreign police officials have reportedly identified similar problems of dissemination of intelligence concerning international terrorism to officials in other countries arising under their national laws.

Complaints have also been raised that the Freedom of Information Act (FOIA) contains ambiguities that call into question the authority of U.S. officials to protect from disclosure confidential information received by the U.S. government from foreign government agencies, especially those below the level of a national agency. Foreign officials have often expressed strong views regarding the extent to which FOIA undermines efforts to gather intelligence and confidence on the part of foreign officials in the intelligence-sharing process. U.S. intelligence officials continue to express concern that FOIA constitutes a threat to the confidentiality of intelligence supplied by foreign intelligence sources, although there is agreement that the situation has improved.

An operational issue that has arisen in the United States is whether a centralized data bank on terrorist activities should be created. Wayne Kerstetter, who wrote guidelines for New York City police dealing with terrorism, has identified the problem:

> . . . this failure to routinely collate the information in the possession of federal agencies imposes inevitable limits on the U.S. capacity to realize the full benefits of the information gathered on terrorist activities and ultimately on the U.S. capacity to respond to the threat of terrorism. This failure also creates the danger of information being in the possession of several agencies which if brought together would be recognized as significant but when dispersed is not. It is unfortunate that having paid the economic and civil-liberties prices in collecting the information, we have not structured our affairs to provide the maximum benefits from the information collected. It is in fact a substantial disservice to ourselves and others.

Resistance to creation of a centralized data bank on terrorism has come from civil liberties organizations that contend such a bank would unduly enhance the government's ability to intrude into the private lives of U.S. citizens. Kerstetter's response is that the proliferation of data bases among a number of government agencies makes proper control of the data so as to ensure protection of privacy rights more difficult. In his view, "the intelligence function is best controlled by careful attention to the articulation of sound operating guidelines and effective enforcement of the rules established," and this is best "facilitated by the centralization of intelligence data bases."

A Conference on Legal Aspects of International Terrorism, sponsored by the Department of State and the Law Enforcement Assistance Administration, with the American Society of International Law, and held on December 13–15, 1978, addressed this issue. At the end of the conference the participants agreed on the following recommendation:

> The Executive Branch of the U.S. Government should consider developing a data base on terrorism by centralizing the collation and analyses of information about terrorists and terrorist activities currently collected by various U.S. agencies. Realistic guidelines should be developed defining what information is to be collected, analyzed, and disseminated to ensure that this activity is kept within appropriate limits. Care should be taken, in consultation with Congress, to ensure that appropriate legal authority has been established for this action and that effective guidelines for the activity are promulgated.

To our knowledge, no action has been taken on this recommendation.

Substantive Criminal Law

As we shall see later in this chapter, the United Nations and its specialized agencies have adopted a number of anti-terrorist conventions. Under these conventions a state party is obligated—if it does not extradite a person accused of committing a crime covered by a convention—to submit that person to its own authorities for purposes of prosecution. To fulfill its obligation to be able to prosecute such persons, even if they commit their crimes outside of its territory, the United States has adopted legislation covering aircraft hijacking and sabotage, attacks against internationally protected persons, the taking of hostages, and the theft of nuclear material. The United States is also likely to adopt legislation that will cover attacks in passenger lounges of international airports, the hijacking of or other attacks against ships, and attacks against fixed platforms on the continental shelf—all acts covered by recently concluded conventions.

This legislation normally does not require that the crime have a terrorist dimension to be covered. The legislation on the taking of hostages, however, requires that the hostage taking be done "in order to compel a third person or a governmental organization to do or abstain from doing any act as an explicit or implicit condition for the release of the person detained."

In 1986 the United States broke new ground with the passage of the Omnibus Diplomatic Security and Anti-terrorism Act, which provides U.S. criminal jurisdiction over the killing of, or an act of physical violence with intent to cause serious bodily injury to or that results in such injury to, a U.S. national outside the United States. Although the relevant chapter of the Act is entitled "Extra-territorial Jurisdiction Over Terrorist Acts Abroad Against United States Nationals," there is no requirement that the killing or violent act include the traditional elements of a terrorist act. Instead, the legislation incorporates the element of terrorism as a limitation on prosecutorial discretion:

> (e) LIMITATION ON PROSECUTION.—No prosecution for any offense described in this section shall be undertaken by the United States except on written certification of the Attorney General or the highest ranking subordinate of the Attorney General with responsibility for criminal prosecutions that, in the judgment of the

certifying official, such offense was intended to coerce, intimidate, or retaliate against a government or a civilian population.

The conference report on the Act makes it clear that the certification of the Attorney General or his designate is final and not subject to judicial review. The conference report also clarifies the meaning of the term "civilian population" by noting that it "includes a general population as well as other specific identifiable segments of society such as the membership of a religious faith or of a particular nationality. . . ." It is not necessary that either the targeted government or the civilian population be that of the United States.

In an earlier version, the Omnibus Diplomatic Security and Anti-terrorism Act of 1986 had a reference to terrorism as an element of the offense itself. The reasons why this was dropped in the final version of the Act are enlightening.

These reasons have been nicely summarized by Geoffrey Levitt, formerly an attorney in the Office of the Legal Adviser, Department of State, who worked on the Act. Levitt first suggests that the political intent element characteristic of a "generic" definition of terrorism is inherently vague and then states:

> In the U.S. legal context, this flaw poses fundamental constitutional problems. The due process clause requires that criminal statutes "give a person of ordinary intelligence fair warning that his contemplated conduct is forbidden by the statute." When first amendment concerns are also involved, as they would of necessity be in any statute that included a politically oriented intent element, this requirement has even greater force. Even were such problems somehow resolved, the breadth of a generic intent element would severely complicate the task of prosecutors, who would be required to prove beyond a reasonable doubt the presence of a particular political motivation. Consequently, this would leave the Government open to accusations of selective prosecution based on the political views of defendants. A separate but substantial problem would be the likely absence of a similar intent element in the penal law of extradition treaty partners, thus removing the factor of dual criminality, a prerequisite to extradi-

tion—and one must wonder what the point would be of an international terrorism offense for which the United States could not successfully request the extradition of suspected offenders. . . .

Some have claimed that the Act is fatally flawed because it relies on the passive personality principle of criminal jurisdiction—i.e., the nationality of the victim—a principle that the United States has traditionally rejected as not supported by international law. This legislation, however, is arguably supported by other principles of international law. For example, despite some judicial opinion in the United States to the contrary, substantial authority exists for the proposition that international terrorism is subject to the universality principle of criminal jurisdiction, i.e., it is a crime against the world community in general and any country that obtains custody over a terrorist can prosecute him for his crime. In congressional hearings, moreover, the Legal Adviser to the U.S. Department of State cited the protective principle of jurisdiction in support of the legality of the legislation. Under the protective principle, a state "has jurisdiction to prescribe a rule of law attaching legal consequences to conduct outside its territory that threatens its security as a state or the operation of its governmental functions, provided the conduct is generally recognized as a crime under the law of states that have reasonably developed legal systems." Attacks intended to coerce, intimidate, or retaliate against a government or a civilian population would normally threaten either U.S. national security or such governmental operations as the conduct of foreign policy or the furtherance of international trade. Judicious application of this legislation should therefore refute any claims that the United States is violating international law.

Economic Sanctions

The United States has long been the Olympic champion with respect to the imposition of economic sanctions for political ends. Since the early 1970s, moreover, economic sanctions have been a prominent part of the U.S. response to foreign involvement in international terrorism. Numerous congressional statutes authorize or require the executive branch to limit various economic relationships with countries the Secretary of State has determined to be supporters of terrorism. At this writing this group includes Libya, North Korea, Syria, South Yemen, Iran, Iraq, and Cuba.

Recently, the United States has intensified the use of economic retaliation against states it deems to be sponsors of international terrorism. President Reagan's national emergency declaration of January 1986 prohibited virtually all economic transactions with Libya and froze Libyan assets subject to U.S. jurisdiction. Similarly, the United States tightened controls on exports to Iran in 1984 and strengthened sanctions against Syria in November 1986 and June 1987, although none of these sanctions was as sweeping as those imposed against Libya.

On the whole the United States has applied these sanctions unilaterally. To be sure, some Western European states also have applied economic sanctions against Libya and Syria, but these efforts have been modest.

The United States and its allies (as well as the Soviet Union) have recently applied severe economic sanctions against Iraq. These sanctions, however, were applied because of Iraq's invasion of Kuwait, not because of its support of terrorism, although the Bush administration added Iraq to its list of state sponsors of terrorism. Moreover, it is worth noting that the sanctions applied to Iraq were taken pursuant to a UN Security Council resolution that created a legal obligation on UN member states to impose such sanctions.

The use of economic sanctions against states that the United States has deemed to be sponsors of terrorism has been controversial, and we will consider some of the issues that have arisen later in this chapter.

In the USSR, legislative norms encompassing criminal responsibility for acts of terrorism are embodied in All-union (federal) laws and in the criminal codes of each union republic. Union-republican codes in practice reproduce the corresponding norms of federal legislation. All-union or republican laws exclusively devoted to terrorism do not exist in the Soviet Union.

In accordance with ongoing legal and judicial reform movement in the USSR, criminal legislation is under review. Draft Fundamentals for criminal legislation for the USSR and Union republics were published at the end of 1988 and are currently under public discussion. At the appropriate time that draft legislation will be considered by the USSR Supreme Soviet, the legislative body in the Soviet Union.

An outstanding characteristic of this draft law is that it both takes account of the international dimensions of several types of criminal acts, and establishes individual criminal responsibility in national law for those acts international in character. "Soviet criminal legislation," it says in the draft, "contributes to the struggle with crimes against peace and the security of mankind and to the strengthening of cooperations among nations." Crime, according to the draft law, is a socially dangerous act (action or inaction), which encroaches not only on human individuals or state establishments or a country's law and order, but also "on the peace and security of mankind." Such a general reference to peace and the security of mankind as an object of criminal encroachments is novel in the fundamental criminal legislation of the USSR. That much is surely expected to be approved by the USSR Supreme Soviet.

However, until new criminal legislation is enacted, the Fundamentals of criminal legislation of the USSR and Union republics adopted in 1958 will remain in force. Adopted on this basis in the same year, there is the law on criminal responsibility for state crimes. Among these crimes are two which touch on terrorism: "terrorist's acts" (Article 3) and "terrorist's acts against the representative of a foreign state" (Article 4). Both of these crimes belong to the category of particularly dangerous state crimes and the Fundamentals also qualify them as serious.

Along with these two laws there are a number of other legislative acts relating to terrorism, including international terrorism. These acts include the following decrees of the Presidium of the USSR Supreme Soviet: "On the criminal responsibility for hijacking an airliner" (1973); "On strengthening punishments for the illegal transport of flammable materials or explosives by air" (1973); "On punishments for illegal carrying, acquisition, manufacture and sale of firearms, ammunition and explosives" (1974); "On the criminal responsibility for the taking of hostages" (1987); and "On the criminal responsibility for unlawful action with radioactive materials" (1988). Embodied in all of these federal legislative acts, norms on criminal responsibility are incorporated in the criminal codes of the Union republics, and it is the articles of these codes that are the basis for the judicial punishment of those found guilty of acts of terrorism.

Under the current legislation, what are understood to be terrorist acts in general and terrorist acts against representatives of foreign governments?

Terrorist acts are understood to be, first, the murder of state or public officials or other representatives of power, carried out in cooperation with their state or public activity, with the goal of undermining or weakening Soviet power; second, inflicting serious, bodily injury on someone from among this group of people. Since the alleged perpetrators of these crimes can be not only citizens of the USSR but also foreigners, the relevant article of the law on criminal responsibility for "terrorist's acts" encompasses this particular variety of international terrorism.

Other varieties of international terrorism are directly addressed by the article of the law which speaks of terrorist acts against the representatives of foreign governments. Such acts consist of murder of such a representative "with the goal of provoking war or international complications" or inflicting serious bodily injury on him with such a goal. The international character of such a terrorist act is not obviated if the alleged perpetrator is a citizen of the USSR or an individual without citizenship residing within the borders of the USSR.

Thus, the 1958 law permits criminal punishment not only for acts of terror having a strictly domestic character, but also for certain varieties of international terrorism.

Because of their dangerous character and consequences, explosions, arson, and other actions carried out with the goal of weakening the Soviet state and designed for the mass destruction of people, inflicting bodily harm or other losses of health are similar to terrorist acts, although in the law they are called sabotage. The main difference between those crimes and strictly terrorist acts is that the quantity of deaths from the crime of sabotage must be significant, as one of the consequences must be not simply the destruction of people but their "mass destruction." And here are meant ordinary people, not necessarily state or public officials.

The 1958 law also includes in the category of especially dangerous state crimes any organized activity directed toward carrying out such a crime, including both of the varieties of terrorist acts noted above and sabotage, as well as their preparation and the creation of organizations having as their goal the execution of such crimes.

Other state crimes, though not among the especially dangerous, include:

—withholding information about individuals preparing for or executing the crimes listed above;
—premeditated agreement to cover up such a crime.

Criminal penalties for these crimes of terrorism range from ten to fifteen years imprisonment with confiscation of all possessions, and exile for two to five years, to the death penalty with confiscation of all possessions, if the terrorist's acts resulted in death for the victim of the crime. If serious bodily injury was inflicted on the victim, the minimum term of imprisonment is eight years, but the death penalty does not apply. Appropriate penalties are applied to organizational activities directed toward instigating or committing acts of terrorism or sabotage or preparing for them (the minimum imprisonment is ten years). Withholding information about these crimes, as well as premediated conspiracy to conceal them, is punishable by one to three years imprisonment, or two years of hard labor.

Another criminal activity characterized by Soviet law as a terrorist act is a public call "to commit a terrorist act or sabotage." This crime is defined by a decree of a Presidium of the USSR Supreme Soviet of April 8, 1988, amending the USSR law about criminal responsibility for crimes against the state, and is punishable by imprisonment for a term up to three years or by a fine up to 3,000 rubles.

Aircraft hijacking, which in international practice is identified with acts of terrorism, is punishable in the USSR in accordance with a specially enacted law—the USSR Supreme Soviet Presidium decree on criminal responsibility for hijacking. Under this law, the following acts are punishable:

—The hijacking of an aircraft, either on land or during flight. (Punishable by imprisonment from 3–10 years.)
—The hijacking of an aircraft, either on land or during flight, as well as the capturing of the aircraft with the intention of hijacking, "if resulting in an accident or some other serious consequences." (Punishable by imprisonment of 5–15 years, with or without the confiscation of all possessions.)

If any of the criminal acts listed above "resulted in heavy bodily injury or death," it is punishable by imprisonment from eight to fifteen years with confiscation of all possessions, or by the death penalty with confiscation of all possessions.

The decree on criminal responsibility for air hijacking also provides punishment for premediated harboring of a criminal (imprisonment of up to five years, or two years hard labor), as well as for witholding information about known acts of hijacking, either committed or in the state of planning (imprisonment for up to three years, or two years of hard labor).

In order to enhance the effectiveness of the effort to combat terrorism and hijacking, criminal responsibility has been introduced for two kinds of actions which terrorists often engage in before committing their "major" crimes. First, it is a crime to bear, keep, buy, manufacture, or sell firearms (hunting rifles are exempted), ammunition, and explosives—if there is no special permission. This is punishable by a prison term of up to five years (the decree of 1974). This decree also states that individuals who voluntarily surrender firearms, ammunition, and explosives they illegally possess are exempted from criminal responsibility.

Second, it is a crime for aircraft passengers to carry any explosive or flammable substance in the luggage or otherwise (the decree of 1973). This crime is punishable by imprisonment of up to three years, or two years of hard labor, or by up to 200 rubles. If these actions cause serious damage, they are punishable by imprisonment for from three to ten years.

Soviet criminal legislation is also responsive to new dimensions of the fight against international terrorism, including such "modern" manifestations as nuclear terrorism, In March 1988, the Soviet Union acceded to the International Convention on Physical Protection of Nuclear Materials. The Presidium of the USSR Supreme Soviet in this connection passed the decree "On criminal responsibility for unlawful action with radioactive materials." Establishing criminal responsibility for this action not only provides the legislative basis necessary to implement this international agreement accepted by the Soviet Union, but also recognizes the "special danger which the unlawful actions with the radioactive materials presents." The quoted passage of this decree demonstrates the concern that the Soviet legislature has about duly protecting the people's life and health against the hazards involved in handling nuclear material.

Among the criminally punishable actions which fall under the provisions of this law, the Supreme Soviet decree first lists the threat to steal radioactive materials "with the purpose to blackmail the state, international organization, natural or judicial person to commit any action or to refrain from committing it if there was reason to believe that the threat was real." Punishment is imprisonment for up to three years.

Under the decree, it is also a crime to threaten to use radioactive materials "with the purpose to cause physical destruction of the people or some other serious consequences if there was a reason to think that this threat was real." This type of threat is punishable by imprisonment of up to five years.

Also relevant to the fight against nuclear terrorism is the rule in the decree which established criminal responsibility for the "violations of regulations of the keeping, use, accounting and transportation of radioactive materials, as well as the other rules to handle them if these actions can cause the death of people or some other serious consequences." Such violations are punishable by imprisonment of up to three years, or up to two years hard labor, or by a 300-ruble fine. If such violations "caused the death of people, or other serious consequences," they can be punished by imprisonment of up to ten years.

Under Soviet law, another type of criminal act which is identified with terrorist activity is the taking of hostages. In 1987, when acceding to the 1979 International Convention Against the Taking of Hostages, the USSR in its instrument of accession included a special declaration to the effect that the Union of Soviet Socialist Republics condemns international terrorism which takes innocent human lives, jeopardizes fundamental freedoms and personal inviolability, and destabilizes the international situation, whatever motivations terrorist acts may have.

Following the accession to the convention, the Presidium of the Supreme Soviet enacted in the same year the above-mentioned decree on the criminal responsibility for the taking of hostages. Pursuant to the convention, the decree made punishable seizure or detention of a person as a hostage if those acts are coupled with the threat to kill, to inflict bodily injury, or to continue detention of that person in order to compel a state, an international organization, natural or judicial person, or a group thereof, to do or abstain from doing any act as a condition for the release of the hostage.

The punishment for the offense is imprisonment for up to ten years. If those acts resulted in serious consequences, the punishment is from five to fifteen years of imprisonment, with or without confiscation of possessions.

The provisions set forth above are, however, not applicable if the offense of hostage taking is committed within the USSR territory when the perpetrator who has taken or detained a hostage is also within that territory and both the offender and the hostage are USSR nationals. This is covered by relevant Soviet domestic legislation.

The world community has responded to international terrorism in a number of ways. The most formal legal response has been the conclusion of international agreements designed to combat various manifestations of international terrorism. Less legal in form, although raising legal issues, is the imposition of sanctions upon states that support international terrorism. Such sanctions have been applied in accordance with informal political consensus.

The responses have been global, regional, bilateral, or unilateral in character. Our focus is on the global anti-terrorist conventions because these are the treaties that both the United States and the Soviet Union have ratified. In addition, in 1986, the United States and the Soviet Union amended a bilateral Air Transport Services Agreement to incorporate a model aviation security article, and this will be briefly discussed. Although the Soviet Union is not a party to the Bonn Declaration, and the United States and the Soviet Union do not currently have a bilateral agreement on aviation hijacking along the lines of the United States-Cuba Memorandum of Understanding on Hijacking of Aircraft and Vessels and Other Offenses, both of these legal responses will be addressed because of the possibility that they might serve as guides to future U.S.-Soviet cooperation in combatting terrorism.

To date, the world community has adopted eight global anti-terrorist conventions: the Convention on Offenses and Certain Other Acts Committed on Board Aircraft (Tokyo Convention), the Convention for the Suppression of Unlawful Seizure of Aircraft (Hague Convention), the Convention for the Suppression of Unlawful Acts Against the Safety of Civil Aviation (Montreal Convention), the Convention for the Suppression of Unlawful Acts of Violence at Airports Serving International Civil Aviation (Montreal Protocol), the Convention on Prevention and Punishment of Crimes Against Internationally Protected Persons, Including Diplomatic Agents (Convention on Protected Persons), the International Convention Against the Taking of Hostages (Hostages Convention), the Convention for the Suppression of Unlawful Acts Against the Safety of Maritime Navigation (IMO Convention), and the Protocol for the Suppression of Unlawful Acts Against the Safety of Fixed Platforms Located on the Continental Shelf (IMO Protocol). The United States and the Soviet Union are parties to the Hague Convention, the Montreal Convention, the Convention on Protected Persons, the Hostages Convention, and the Tokyo Convention. The Montreal Protocol, the IMO Convention, and the IMO Protocol, having only recently been concluded, are not yet in force.

All these conventions seek to suppress international terrorism by establishing a framework for international cooperation among states. To accomplish this goal, the Convention on Protected Persons, for example, requires states parties (1) to cooperate in order to prevent, within their territories, preparation for attacks on diplomats within or outside their territories, (2) to exchange information, and (3) to coordinate administrative measures against such attacks. If an attack against an internationally protected person takes place and an alleged offender has fled the country where the attack occurred, states parties are to cooperate in the exchange of information concerning the circumstances of the crime and the alleged offender's identity and whereabouts. Any state party where the alleged offender is found is obliged to take measures to ensure his presence for purposes of extradtion or prosecution and to inform interested states and international organizations of the measures taken. Finally, parties are to cooperate in assisting criminal proceedings brought for attacks on internationally protected persons. This imposes, inter alia, an obligation on the state party to supply all relevant evidence at its disposal.

A key feature of these conventions is the requirement that a state party that apprehends an alleged offender in its territory either extradite him or submit his case to its own authorities for purposes of prosecution. Strictly speaking, none of these conventions alone creates an obligation to extradite; by requiring the submission of alleged offenders for prosecution if extradition fails, they contain an inducement to extradite. Moreover, a legal basis for extradition is provided either in the convention or through incorporation of the offenses mentioned in the convention into existing or future extradition treaties between the parties. To varing degrees, the conventions also obligate the parties to take the important practical step of attempting to apprehend the accused and hold him in custody.

The most important goal of these provisions is to ensure prosecution of the accused. To this end, the conventions state quite strongly the alternative obligation either to extradite or to submit the accused for prosecution. The obligation, however, is not to try the accused, much less to punish him, but to submit the case to be considered for prosecution by the appropriate national prosecuting authority. If the prosecuting state's criminal justice system lacks integrity, the risk of political intervention in the prosecution or at trial exists. Such intervention may prevent the trial or conviction of the accused, or act as a mitigating influence at the sentencing stage.

Even when the prosecuting state's criminal justice system functions with integrity, it may be very difficult to obtain the evidence necessary to convict the accused when the alleged offense was committed in another country. This very practical impediment to conviction can be removed only by patient and sustained efforts to develop and expand "judicial assistance" and other forms of cooperation between the law enforcement and judicial systems of different countries. The conventions create an obligation to cooperate in this regard, but such an obligation is often difficult for countries with different types of legal systems to meet, even assuming that they act in good faith.

The Hostages Convention adds a new dimension to existing international legal measures to combat terrorism. The convention seeks to ensure that international acts of hostage taking will be covered either by the Hostages Convention itself or by one of the applicable conventions on the law of armed conflict. The Hostages Convention also constitutes a partial rejection of the contention that acts of terrorism are permissible if committed as part of a war of national liberation. Under its Article 12, the convention shall not apply to an act of hostage taking committed in the course of armed conflict as defined in the Geneva Conventions of 1949 and the Protocol thereto, including armed conflicts mentioned in Article I, paragraph 4, of Additional Protocol I of 1977, in which peoples are fighting against colonial domination and alien occupation and against racist regimes in exercise of their right of self-determination.

The United States and the Soviet Union are also parties to two other multilateral conventions which, while not directed expressly against terrorism, serve a similar purpose. The Convention on the Prohibition of the Development, Production and Stockpiling of Bacteriological (Biological) and Toxic Weapons and on Their Destruction prohibits the development, production, or stockpiling of microbiological and biological agents (weapons) that are of potential use to terrorists. Similarly, the recently concluded Convention on the Physical Protection of Nuclear Materials (Convention on Nuclear Materials) prevents parties from exporting or importing or authorizing the export or import of nuclear material used for peaceful purposes, unless they give assurances that such material will be protected at prescribed levels during international transport. The Convention on Nuclear Materials also provides a framework for international cooperation in the recovery and protection of stolen nuclear materials, and requires that states parties make certain serious offenses involving nuclear material punishable, and that they extradite or prosecute offenders.

The effectiveness of these global conventions as far as the task of complete elimination of terrorist activities in all their forms and manifestations is concerned is far from being adequate. Even if fully implemented, the limited and piecemeal solutions of these conventions would be of no use in combatting the many manifestations of terrorism not covered by the conventions. For example, they do not cover attacks on international business persons, a common tactic of international terrorism. Similarly, they do not criminalize bombings and other violent attacks against civilians, an increasingly prevalent strategem of international terrorists. Moreover, existing global conventions have not been effectively implemented. To be sure, there have been some successes. Since the conclusion of the International Civil Aviation Conventions (ICAO Conventions) there has been a general decline in aircraft hijacking. This decline is due in part to the preventive techniques mandated by those conventions and now employed both in airports and aboard aircraft. There is also ample evidence that hijackers have been submitted for prosecution either in the states where they have been found or in states to which they have been extradited.

The record has been uneven, however. On June 14, 1985, Shi'ite Muslim hijackers commandeered TWA Flight 847 just after it took off from Athens carrying 145 passengers and eight crew members; the hijackers forced the pilot to fly to Beirut. One passenger, a U.S. Navy diver, was killed. The hijackers released the rest of the captives in stages; the last group, all U.S. nationals, were freed on June 30, 1985.

Lebanon never prosecuted the hijackers. Nor was it under any obligation to do so. Although both Lebanon and the United States are parties to the Hague Convention, there is no extradition treaty in force between the two countries, and the U.S. government declined to make the request for extradition of the hijackers that would have triggered Lebanon's obligation under the Hague Convention either to extradite the hijackers or to submit them to prosecution. Apparently a number of extraneous factors, such as concern for other U.S. citizens held hostage in Lebanon, contributed to the decision not to request extradition, although the United States, as a policy matter, had declined to request extradition from a country with which it does not have a bilateral extradition treaty.

There have been some successes in prosecuting those who engage in attacks against internationally protected persons, especially diplomats, but the record is mixed. Also, the number of countries that are parties to the Convention on Protected Persons remains disappointingly small. The experience to date under the Hostages Convention is not quite a happy one, as illustrated by the failure to bring to justice the perpetrators who allegedly masterminded the hijacking of the Italian cruise ship *Achille Lauro*, which resulted in the death of Leon Klinghoffer, a U.S. citizen in a wheelchair.

A major difficulty with the anti-terrorist conventions is that, with the exception of the Hague Convention on aircraft hijacking, there are insufficient data on the extent to which persons who have committed crimes covered by the conventions have been subjected to extradition, prosecution, and punishment for their crimes. In the case of aircraft hijacking, the U.S. Federal Aviation Administration keeps excellent records. This is not the case, however, with respect to the other crimes covered by the anti-terrorist conventions.

Most of the global anti-terrorist conventions have relatively strong dispute settlement provisions that allow for binding arbitration or adjudication of disputes that arise between states parties regarding the interpretation or application of the conventions. However, some of them permit a party to "opt out" in accordance with a reservation made at the time it became a party. The Soviet Union has also made such reservations, but since 1987 it has been in the process of reconsidering its position, as may be exemplified by the USSR acceptance of the compulsory jurisdiction of the International Court of Justice on human rights treaties. Moreover, none of these conventions provides for economic or other sanctions against states that offer haven or other assistance to terrorists.

The first efforts in September 1973 to conclude an independent sanctions convention for the ICAO Conventions at the Rome Security Conference and at the ICAO Extraordinary Assembly were unsuccessful. Other efforts to conclude a sanctions convention have met with a similar fate. Efforts in the ICAO having failed, an initiative outside the United Nations was undertaken. On July 17, 1978, the heads of state and government participating in the Bonn Economic Summit (Canada, France, the Federal Republic of Germany, Italy, Japan, the United Kingdom, and the United States—known as the Summit Countries) agreed upon a declaration which has come to be known as the Bonn Declaration on Hijacking. The Declaration provides:

> The Heads of State and Government, concerned about terrorism and the taking of hostages, declare that their governments will intensify their joint efforts to combat international terrorism. To this end, in cases where a country refuses extradition or prosecution of those who have hijacked an aircraft and/or does not return such aircraft, the Heads of State and Government are jointly resolved that their governments shall take immediate action to cease all flights to that country. At the same time, their governments will initiate action to halt all in-coming flights from that country, or from any country of the airlines of the country concerned. They urge other governments to join them in the commitment.

Although there is some disagreement on this point, most commentators agree that the Bonn Declaration is not a binding legal instrument, but rather a statement of policy which expresses the intent of the Summit Countries to take action when, subsequent to a hijacking, other states have failed to live up to their obligations with regard to it. Follow-up efforts have succeeded in obtaining widespread support for the Declaration and in inducing additional countries to become parties to the ICAO Conventions. The Soviet Union has not yet adhered to the principles of the Bonn Declaration.

By exchange of notes on February 13, 1986, the United States and the Soviet Union agreed to insertion of the following article in the Air Transport Services Agreement of November 4, 1966:

Article 6 *bis*

(1) Consistent with rights otherwise enjoyed under international law, the Contracting Parties reaffirm that their obligation to protect the security of civil aviation against acts of

unlawful interference forms an integral part of this Agreement.

(2)   The Contracting Parties shall provide all necessary aid to each other to prevent acts of unlawful seizure of aircraft and other unlawful acts against the safety of aircraft, airports and air navigation facilities and any other threat to aviation security.

(3)   The Contracting Parties shall act in full conformity with the provisions of the Convention for the Suppression of Unlawful Seizure of Aircraft, signed at The Hague on 16 December 1970 and the Convention for the Suppression of Acts Against the Safety of Civil Aviation, signed at Montreal on 23 September 1971.

(4)   The Contracting Parties shall act in full conformity with the aviation security provisions and regulations established by the International Civil Aviation Organization and designated as Annexes to the Convention on International Civil Aviation; they shall require that operators of aircraft of their registry or operators who have their principal place of business or permanent residence in their territory, and the operators of airports in their territory act in conformity with such aviation security provisions.

(5)   Each Contracting Party agrees to observe the security provisions required by the other Contracting Party for entry into the territory of the other Contracting Party to take adequate measures to protect aircraft and inspect passengers, their carry-on items as well as cargo and aircraft stores prior to and during boarding or loading. Each Contracting Party shall also give sympathetic consideration to any request from the other Contracting Party for special security measures, to meet a particular threat.

(6)   When an incident or threat of an incident of unlawful seizure of aircraft or other unlawful acts against the safety of passengers, crew, airports and air navigation facilities occurs, the Contracting Parties shall assist each other by facilitating communications and other appropriate measures intended to terminate rapidly and safely such incident or threat thereof.

(7)   When a Contracting Party has reasonable grounds to believe that the other Contracting Party has departed from the aviation security provision of this Article, the aeronautical authorities of the first Contracting Party may request immedi-

ate consultations with the aeronautical authorities of that
Contracting Party. Failure to reach a satisfactory agreement
within 15 days from the date of the request for consultations,
or an urgent threat to the security of international civil aviation, will constitute grounds for application of Article 5 of
this Agreement."

Article 5 relates to grounds for termination of the agreement; it has not been necessary to invoke this provision. On
the contrary, the United States and the Soviet Union, with
increasing success, have cooperated pursuant to the terms of
Article 6 *bis.*

In addition to the global multilateral conventions against
terrorism discussed above, there are several bilateral agreements specifically directed against aircraft hijacking or the
hijacking of ships. Perhaps the most interesting example of
such bilateral agreements is the United States-Cuba Memorandum of Understanding on Hijacking of Aircraft and Vessels and Other Offenses. It provides that any person who hi-
jacks an aircraft or vessel registered under the law of one party
to the territory of the other party shall either be returned to
the party of registry or "be brought before the courts of the
party whose territory he reached for trial in conformity with
its laws for the offense punishable by the most severe penalty
according to the cirsumstances and seriousness of the acts to
which the Article refers." Thus, the memorandum incorporates the extradite or prosecute formula, but does so in a more
meaningful way than do the multilateral anti-terrorist conventions. Unlike the multilateral conventions, the United States-
Cuba Memorandum requires that the accused actually be
tried and not merely submitted "for the purpose of prosecution."

Under the United States-Cuba Memorandum, each party
expressly recognizes an affirmative obligation to prevent the
use of its territory as a base for committing the illegal acts
covered by the memorandum. Each party must try "with a
view to severe punishment" any person who, "within its territory, hereafter conspires to promote, or promotes, or prepares,

or directs, or forms part of an expedition which from its territory or any other place carries out acts of violence or deprivation against aircraft or vessels of any kind or registration coming from or going to the territory of the other party . . . or carries out such acts or similar unlawful acts in the territory of the other party."

Finally, the United States-Cuba Memorandum severely limits the extent to which the party where the hijacker arrives may take his motivation into account. It provides, in pertinent part, that there may be taken "into consideration any extenuating or mitigating circumstances in those cases in which the persons responsible for the acts were being sought for strictly political reasons and were in real and imminent danger of death without a viable alternative for leaving the country, provided their was no financial extortion or physical injury to the members of the crew, passengers, or other persons in connection with the hijacking."

In 1976, the memorandum was denounced by Cuba on the ground that the United States had failed to control terrorists who had planted a bomb on a Cuban civilian aircraft. Nonetheless, in practice since this time Cuba has shown that hijackers still face imprisonment in Cuba or extradition to the United States.

As we discuss more fully in the next section of this chapter, the U.S.-Cuban Memorandum might serve as a model for a similar bilateral agreement between the United States and the Soviet Union.

The United States and the Soviet Union might jointly take a number of legal initiatives to combat international terrorism. These initiatives are organized under four topic headings: narco-terrorism, i.e., terrorism, closely associated with international drug trafficking; technological terrorism, i.e., terrorism involving weapons of mass destruction, including in particular nuclear, radiological, chemical, and biological weapons; hostage taking and hijacking of aircraft and vessels; and the deliberate targeting of civilians.

Narco-Terrorism

1. THE UNITED STATES AND THE SOVIET UNION SHOULD AC-
TIVELY EXPLORE THE FEASIBILITY OF ESTABLISHING AN IN-
TERNATIONAL CRIMINAL COURT WITH JURIDICTION OVER
INTERNATIONAL DRUG TRAFFICKING, ASSOCIATED ACTS OF
VIOLENCE, AND OTHER ACTS OF INTERNATIONAL TERRORISM.

Proposals to create a permanent international criminal court have been around for quite some time. Subsequent to the Nuremburg and Tokyo trials, which were held before ad hoc international military tribunals, the United Nations began work on a Draft Code of Offenses Against the Peace and Security of Mankind as well as on a draft statute for an international criminal court. Both a draft code and a draft statute for an international crimimial code were produced, but the International Law Commission, a subsidiary body of the UN General Assembly, having resumed its work on the draft code early in the 1982 session, has not yet completed it, and the General Assembly which had discontinued its work on the draft statute in 1954 has not yet reverted to it. Until recently the idea of an international criminal court was regarded by many as of academic interest only. Several developments have stimulated renewed interest in the possibility of an international criminal court.

First, in September 1987, General Secretary Mikhail S. Gorbachev, in his article on the United Nations, circulated as a UN document, suggested that a tribunal should be established under United Nations auspices to investigate acts of international terrorism. Second, in a speech delivered on June 2, 1988, at the United Nations, A. N. R. Robinson, prime minister of Trinidad-Tobago, proposed that the United Nations review existing international criminal codes and consider the possibility of establishing international commissions of inquiry and, in the long run, of creating an international criminal court with jurisdiction over such crimes as, in particular, the use of prohibited weapons and international drug trafficking. By letter of August 21, 1989, the Permanent Representative of Trinidad-Tobago to the United Nations requested that the Secretary-General include as a supplementary item on the agenda of the forty-fourth session of the General Assembly the possibility of establishing an international criminal court with jurisdiction over illicit trafficking in narcotic drugs across national frontiers and other transnational criminal activities. As noted earlier, the matter was referred to the International Law Commission, and the Commission issued a report in September 1990. Third, the U.S. Senate has passed a resolution calling upon the President of the United States to begin discussions with foreign governments on the feasibility of establishing an international criminal court with jurisdiction over the prosecution of persons accused of engaging in international drug trafficking or other international crimes. These developments may reflect a change in attitude that will permit reconsideration of proposals to establish an international criminal court.

There have been a number of proposals of non-governmental organizations or by scholars regarding the establishment of an international criminal court. Most of these envisage a tribunal with jurisdiction over a lengthy list of international crimes and with an elaborate structure, including such subsidiary organs of the court as procurator, public defender, commission of inquiry, prosecutor, board of clemency and parole, or even jail. We would suggest a more modest approach, especially with respect to jurisdiction. That is, member states of the United Nations should explore the feasibility of establishing an international criminal court with jurisdiction only over those crimes covered by the global anti-terrorist conventions and over international drug trafficking.

A discussion of what the statute of such a court might look like is beyond the scope of this chapter. We would note one major problem, however, and that is whether member states of the United Nations would be willing to allow an international criminal court to exercise criminal jurisdiction over their nationals. In the United States, there are serious constitutional issues to be resolved before any such agreement might be forthcoming. In any event we would suggest that in light of such problems, a provision along the lines of Article 27 of the UN's 1953 Revised Draft Statute would be indispensable. Article 27 provides that

> No person shall be tried before the Court unless jurisdiction has been conferred upon the Court by the State or States of which he is a national and by the State or States in which the crime is alleged to have been committed.

The rationale behind Article 27, which still pertains today, is aptly summarized in the Report of the 1953 UN Committee on International Criminal Jurisdiction:

> Some members of the Committee believed that article 27 of the Geneva draft statute covered two quite different problems. The first part of the article, which provided that no national of a State should be tried by the court unless that State had conferred jurisdiction, was a protection of the sovereignty of States and an assurance to them that no trial would take place without their consent. The second part of the article, which provided that jursidiction also must be conferred by the State or States in which the crime was alleged to have been committed, had the purpose of preventing conflicts of jurisdiction between the international criminal court and national courts.

2. *The United States and the Soviet Union should promote cooperation between law enforcement authorities with respect to acts of violence associated with the trade in narcotics, through the International Criminal Police Organization (INTERPOL) or other appropriate international institutions or by way of bilateral consultations.*

Both the United States and the Soviet Union have recognized the grave threat posed by international drug trafficking and have cooperated in efforts to combat it. For example, both countries strongly supported the conclusion of 1988 of the United Nations Convention Against Illicit Traffic in Narcotic Drugs and Psychotropic Substances. Also, on October 10,

1989, the United States and the Soviet Union supported a British initiative to have the UN Security Council declare drug trafficking a "threat to international peace and security" and thus a proper matter for the Council to keep under review in accordance with the UN Charter. The majority of members of the Council opposed the British proposal, however, arguing that it would expand the Security Council's role and encourage it to intervene in problems that do not involve a direct threat to the peace.

This cooperation between the United States and the Soviet Union should continue and intensify. The Soviet Union has recently become a member of INTERPOL and that institution might be a forum for enhanced cooperation between the two countries. U.S.-Soviet cooperation with respect to acts of violence associated with the narcotics trade also can be pursued through other international institutions or by way of bilateral consulations.

Technological Terrorism

1. *The United States and the Soviet Union should make joint efforts, within the United Nations, the International Atomic Energy Agency, and elsewhere, to increase the number of states parties to the Convention on the Physical Protection of Nuclear Materials.*

Both the United States and the Soviet Union are parties to the Convention on the Physical Protection of Nuclear Materials, which was discussed briefly earlier in this chapter. As of January 1, 1989, however, only twenty-five countries had ratified the convention. In light of the increased likelihood that terrorists may attempt to obtain nuclear materials, this is unsatisfactory. Accordingly, the two countries should make joint efforts, in every appropriate forum, including especially the International Atomic Energy Agency, where the convention was concluded, and the United Nations, to induce more countries to become parties to the convention.

2. *The United States and the Soviet Union should initiate and sponsor a draft convention to define terrorism involving weapons of mass destruction, including in particular nuclear, radiological, chemical, and biological weapons, declare it a crime under international law, and obligate states parties to extradite or prosecute those who commit the crime.*

The only manifestation of 'technological terrorism" currently covered by the anti-terrorist conventions is the theft (though not the use) of nuclear materials used for civilian purposes. This constitutes a serious gap in the law. In addition to the nuclear threat, there is increasing evidence of the ready availability of chemical and biological weapons (sometimes described as the poor man's atomic bomb). Accordingly, the United States and the Soviet Union should initiate and sponsor a convention to close this gap in the law and work toward effective cooperative measures to prevent weapons of mass destruction from falling into hands of terrorists, and to ensure their prosecution and punishment if preventive measures fail.

Hostages and Hijacking of Aircraft and Vessels

1. *The United States and the Soviet Union should negotiate a bilateral agreement along the lines of the U.S.-Cuba Memorandum of Understanding on Hijacking of Aircraft and Vessels and Other Offenses.*

The U.S.-Cuba Memorandum of Understanding on Hijacking of Aircraft and Vessels and Other Offenses has been discussed earlier in this chapter. Because there is no U.S.-Soviet bilateral extradition treaty, the United States, under its law and practice, is unable to extradite a person accused of hijacking a Soviet plane or vessel, which is one of the options under the extradite or prosecute formula contained in the Hague Convention for Suppression of Unlawful Seizure of Aircraft and in the recently concluded Convention for the Suppression of Unlawful Acts Against the Safety of Maritime

Navigation. Nor can the United States request extradition of a person accused of hijacking a U.S. aircraft or vessel.

Perhaps the time is not yet ripe for the United States and the Soviet Union to consider concluding a general bilateral extradition agreement. A U.S.-Soviet agreement along the lines of the U.S.-Cuba Memorandum, however, would seem politically feasible and, in light of the experience under the U.S.-Cuba Memorandum, highly appropriate.

It is important to note that, as pointed out earlier, the rights of an accused are fully protected under the U.S.-Cuba Memorandum. At the same time the memorandum strengthens the primary obligation of the anti-terrorism conventions to ensure prosecution of the accused. The memorandum has worked well even though the United States and Cuba do not have diplomatic relations. With the substantial improvement in relations between the United States and the Soviet Union, the prospects for a U.S.-Soviet agreement along the lines of the U.S.-Cuba Memorandum would seem highly favorable.

2. *The United States and the Soviet Union should support an initiative in the United Nations that would establish a committee to oversee implemenation of the International Convention Against the Taking of Hostages.*

As noted earlier in this chapter, mere ratification of the anti-terrorist conventions is not enough. If these conventions are to be useful, they must be used. To this end, as a first step, the United States and Soviet Union should seek to have the UN Security Council establish a committee with responsibility to monitor implementation of the International Convention Against the Taking of Hostages. The committee might fulfill this responsibility by calling for annual reports from states parties to the convention as to the measures they have taken to enforce the convention. Examples of such measures might include the passage of national legislation authorizing domestic courts to exercise jurisdiction over persons accused of hostage taking, as well as actual extraditions or prosecutions of persons accused of this crime. United Nations prac-

tice already knows some instances of establishing a new UN
body to monitor (or entrusting an existing UN body with the
monitoring of) the implementation of international instruments which have no provision of their own for implemenation machinery. If experience with the committee established
to monitor implementation of the Hostages Convention
proved favorable, its jurisdiction might be expanded to monitor implementation of other anti-terrorist conventions.

If it appears that the United Nations is not yet ready to
establish a commiteee to monitor implementation of the Hostages Convention under the auspices of the Security Council,
the United States and the Soviet Union should seek to have
the UN General Assembly establish such a committee. In any
event, the UN Secretariat could be expected to lend assistance
to the committee.

> 3. *The Soviet Union should consider acceding to the Bonn Dec-*
> *laration or applying its principles. Upon such accession the*
> *United States and the Soviet Union should jointly invite*
> *other member states of the United Nations to do the same.*

As indicated earlier in this chapter, the Bonn Declaration is
a political commitment by states to cut off air traffic with
countries that offer safe haven to aircraft hijackers. Although
the United States and its allies have succeeded in obtaining
widespread support for the Declaration, the Soviet Union has
not yet expressed its willingness to accede to the Declaration
or, failing accession, to apply its principles. In the light of the
Soviet Union's strong abhorrence of aircraft hijacking, we believe it should do so. The United States and the Soviet Union
should then jointly undertake to induce other states that have
not yet done so to follow the Soviet Union's lead.

Deliberate Targeting of Civilians

> 1. *The United States and the Soviet Union should initiate and*
> *sponsor a draft convention that would make the deliberate*
> *targeting of the civilian population an international crime.*

As noted earlier, a major gap in coverage of the anti-terrorist conventions is the deliberate targeting of the civilian population. The United States and the Soviet Union should therefore initiate and sponsor a draft convention that would make the deliberate targeting of the civilian population an international crime. We realize that it would not be easy to reach agreement on a convention to cover this crime, especially since deliberate attacks against the civilian population have been a tactic commonly employed by national liberation groups in some regions. It is noteworthy, however, that the deliberate targeting of the civilian population has long been a war crime under the law of armed conflict, and this proposition has been strongly reaffirmed by the 1977 Protocol I to the Geneva Conventions of 1949, which is designed to apply to the activities of at least some favored national liberation groups. It would seem anomalous that the deliberate targeting of civilians should be a war crime in situations covered by the law of armed conflict and give rise to a requirement that states extradite or prosecute persons accused of the crime, yet fall outside the coverage of international law if committed by individuals who are not engaged in armed conflict as defined by international law.

Appendices

Participants in the U.S.-Soviet Task Force to Prevent Terrorism

For the USSR:

1. IGOR BELIAEV—Political Observer, *Literaturnaya Gazeta*

2. VLADIMIR KOUZNETSOV—Editor of Information Department, *Literaturnaya Gazeta*

3. EVGENY LJAKHOV—Ministry of the Interior (MVD); expert on international law

4. OLEG PROUDKOV—Foreign Editor, *Literaturnaya Gazeta;* expert on international law

5. VALENTIN ROMANOV—Institute of World Economy and International Relations, USSR Academy of Sciences; former Soviet ambassador; expert on international law, world economy, and international relations

*6. LT. GEN. (RETIRED) FEODOR SHERBAK—Former Deputy Chairman of KGB's Second Chief Directorate

*Present in Santa Monica only.

7. ANDREY SHOUMIKHIN—Department Head, USA and Canada Institute of USSR Academy of Sciences; Middle East expert

8. GLEB STAROUSHENKO—Corresponding Member of the Soviet Academy of Sciences; Deputy Director of the Africa Institute; expert on international law

9. VLADIMIR VESSENSKY—Chief Editor, *Literaturnaya Gazeta,* English edition

*10. MAJ. GEN. (RETIRED) VALENTIN ZVEZDENKOV—Former Chief of KGB Counter-terrorism

**11. ASLAN H. ABASHIDZE—Lumumba University of Friendship

**12. IGOR P. BLISHENKO—Vice President of Soviet Lawyers' Association

**13. LIDIA A. MADZHARJAN—Ph.D., professor

**14. EVGENY V. MARTINENKO—Lumumba University of Friendship

**15. SERGEI A. ORDZHENIKIDZE—Deputy Director of the Department, Ministry of Foreign Affairs

**16. ALEXANDR D. SABOV—Department Head, *Literaturnaya Gazeta*

**17. DMITRY A. TROFIMOV—Researcher, Institute of World Economy and International Relations

Interpreters:

　　　*Professor Alexandr Shveitser
　　　*Alexandr Tronfue

For the West:

*1. RAY CLINE—President, Global Strategy Council; Former Deputy Director, CIA

---

*Present in Santa Monica only.
**Present in Moscow only.

*2. WILLIAM COLBY—Of Counsel, Donovan, Leisure, Irving & Newton; Former Director, CIA

3. ERIC GROVE—Associate Director, Foundation for International Security; lecturer on terrorism, Royal Naval College, Dartmouth, England; author, *Common Security Programme Studies on Nuclear Weapons in Europe*

4. BRIAN JENKINS—Senior Managing Director at Kroll Associates and former Chairman of the Political Science Department, The RAND Corporation; author, *International Terrorism: A New Mode of Conflict*

5. GEOFFREY KEMP—Senior Associate, Carnegie Endowment for International Peace; former Special Assistant to the President for National Security Affairs and Senior Director for Near East and South Asian Affairs, National Security Council

6. DR. ROBERT KUPPERMAN—Senior Advisor, Center for Strategic and International Studies; co-author, *Terrorism: Threat, Reality, Response*

7. JOHN MARKS—Executive Director, Search for Common Ground; former Foreign Service Officer; co-author, *The CIA and the Cult of Intelligence;* and author, *The Search for the "Manchurian Candidate"*

8. MARGUERITE MILLHAUSER—Former Partner, Steptoe & Johnson; conflict resolution specialist

9. JOHN F. MURPHY—Villanova University Law School; former Chairman of the American Bar Association's Committee on International Institutions Law; author, *Punishing International Terrorists: The Legal Framework for Policy Initiatives* and *State Support of International Terrorism: Legal, Political, and Economic Dimensions*

10. AUGUSTUS RICHARD NORTON—Permanent Associate Professor of Comparative Politics, Department of Social Sciences, U.S. Military Academy; author, *Amal and Shia: Struggle for the Soul of Lebanon;* senior editor, *Studies in Nuclear Terrorism* and *The International Relations of the PLO*

*Present in Santa Monica only.

11. MICHAEL STOHL—Professor of Political Science and Associate Director of International Programs, Purdue University; editor, *The Politics of Terrorism,* and co-editor, *Current Perspectives on International Terrorism*

12. ROBIN WRIGHT—former Middle East Correspondent; author, *Sacred Rage: The Wrath of Militant Islam*

From Search for Common Ground:

* Betsy Cohen
**Rebecca Fox
  Allen Grossman
  Bonnie Pearlman

Interpreters:

* Natalie Latter
* Dwight Roesch

*Present in Santa Monica only.
**Present in Moscow only.

Task Force Recommendations:
Moscow, 1989

. . . In their bilateral relations, as well as their respective relations with all other states, the United States and the Soviet Union should recognize their strong mutual interest in preventing acts of violence, especially acts of terrorism, whatever their motivation, which could lead to larger conflicts.

We the participants of this meeting recognize that the most serious threats of terrorism involve:

- terrorist incidents that could provoke nuclear confrontation
- terrorist incidents that could provoke warfare or armed conflict
- terrorist incidents that could involve mass casualties, including nuclear, chemical or biological incidents.

We further recognize that the most likely threats of terrorism involve an array of common terrorist tactics that affect both the US and USSR and include:

- attacks on civil aviation including the sabotage of aircraft and hijacking of aircraft
- attacks on ships and platforms and the mining of sea lanes

- attacks on internationally recognized protected persons (e.g., diplomats, children).

Therefore, the United States and the Soviet Union should work together in a manner consistent with general principles of international law to prevent terrorism and control its consequences where it occurs. The issue of international terrorism—its causes, manifestations and consequences—should be high on their bilateral agenda.

In consideration thereof, the participants in the meeting recommend to our respective governments:

1. The creation of a standing bilateral group and channel of communications for the exchange of information pertinent to terrorism. This would provide a designated link for conveying requests and relaying information during a crisis created by a terrorist incident.
2. The provision of mutual assistance (information, diplomatic assistance, technical assistance, etc.), when requested, in the investigation or resolution of terrorist incidents.
3. The prohibition of the sale or transfer of military explosives and certain classes of weapons (to be designated in bilateral discussion between the Soviet and American governments) to non-government organizations; and the restriction and increased controls on the sale or transfer of military explosives and the same classes of weapons to states.
4. The initiation of bilateral discussions to explore the utility of requiring the addition of chemical or other types of "tags" to commercial and military explosives to make them more easily detectable and to aid in the investigation of terrorist bombings.
5. The initiation of joint efforts to prevent terrorists from acquiring chemical, biological, nuclear, or other means of mass destruction. (For example, the 1980 Vienna Convention on the Protection of Nuclear Material.)
6. Consistent with the national security interests as defined by each nation, the exchange of technology that may be useful in preventing or combatting terrorism.
7. The conduct of joint exercises and simulations for the purpose of exploring and developing further means of Soviet-American cooperation during terrorist threats or incidents.
8. In order to strengthen implementation of existing antiterrorism conventions:

(a) The U.S. and the USSR should establish a bilateral group to review the effectiveness of these conventions as instruments for the apprehension, prosecution and punishment of persons who commit the crimes, covered by the Conventions.

(b) The U.S. and the USSR should jointly or individually initiate efforts toward the UN Security Council establishing a Standing Committee on International Terrorism to perform a similar function on a multilateral basis.

9. In order to fill the gaps that exist in current international law and institutions regarding international terrorism:

(a) The U.S. and the USSR should propose the drafting of an international convention that would cover threats and acts of violence that deliberately target the civilian population and that have an international dimension.

(b) The Security Council Standing Committee on International Terrorism referred to above in 1(b) should study and recommend to the Security Council effective measures to ensure that neither military nuclear weapons nor nuclear material designed for civilian use ever get in the hands of terrorists.

(c) Disputes concerning the interpretation and application of the antiterrorist conventions should, if not settled by other means, be referred to the International Court of Justice for resolution.

(d) Renewed consideration should be given to the feasibility of an international tribunal—either *ad hoc* or having a permanent status—to try persons accused of acts of international terrorism.

Recommendations of the Information Working Group:
Santa Monica, September 1989

RAY CLINE
WILLIAM COLBY
JOHN MARKS
IGOR BELIAEV
OLEG PROUDKOV

LT. GEN. (RETIRED) FEO-
DOR SHERBAK
MAJ. GEN. (RETIRED) VA-
LENTIN ZVEZDENKOV

Whereas President George Bush and Soviet Foreign Minister Shevardnadze have emphatically stressed in their speeches before the United Nations how important it is for all nations to work to suppress international terrorism of all kinds, whether conducted by political, religious, and ethnic groups or by narcotics distributors and other criminal gangs; and whereas the danger to the fabric of civilization is tremendous and morally reprehensible, particularly when terrorists deliberately target the general public and innocent bystanders in order to create widespread fear and intimidate authorities into acquiescing in terrorist demands, it is the view of the Soviet and American participants in the Information Working Group (whose names appear above) that:

1. No nation nor any of its government services nor representatives should engage in or sponsor, support, encourage, train, or supply any kind of terrorist act.
2. Nations that condemn terrorism are morally obligated to take all appropriate measures to prevent acts of terrorism and to persuade all nations and subnational groups with which they

have any contact to cease and desist from employing terrorist tactics.

3. Our two nations should establish appropriate liaison and communications channels to discuss the character and origin of terrorist incidents when from time to time they occur.

4. No nation should provide groups that have engaged in terrorist acts with weapons of mass destruction (nuclear, chemical or biological) or high-technology devices such as heat-seeking anti-aircraft missiles or plastic explosives virtually impossible to detect of the kind used to destroy Pan American Flight 103 over Scotland.

5. Direct contact between the intelligence agencies/special services of our two nations should be established for the sole and exclusive purpose of timely exchange of information about terrorist groups or individuals, their tactics, plans, specific operations, supply, training, and support structures.

Recommendations of the Practical Measures Working Group:
Santa Monica, September 1989

Members:

ALLEN GROSSMAN
BRIAN JENKINS
ROBERT KUPPERMAN
MICHAEL STOHL

VLADIMIR KOUZNETSOV
GLEB STAROUSHENKO
VLADIMIR VESSENSKY

PREAMBLE

The working group is aware that combatting terrorism is a long process and will require the cooperation of all nations, but people are being killed now. Thus, we cannot postpone cooperation against terrorists until all global issues that may contribute to the rise of terrorism are resolved. Therefore, with this understanding, we recommend these practical measures, which can be implemented now.

Protection of Civil Aviation

There is already considerable international agreement on efforts to protect civil aviation, for example, the Hague, Tokyo, and Montreal Conventions. Building upon these agreements, we recommend that the U.S. and USSR take the following additional measures:

1. Jointly provide assistance to improve security of ICAO member countries in accordance with objectives identified by the ICAO.

2. Provide mutual assistance in the investigation of incidents of aircraft sabotage.
3. Exchange explosives-detection technology and equipment.
4. Initiate joint Soviet-American efforts to recover portable surface-to-air missiles that are in the hands of non-state actors or on the black market; urge other countries to assist in this recovery and to cease the distribution of portable precision-guided munitions

Efforts to Combat Narco-Terrorism

The violence associated with the drug traffic is an emerging form of terrorism. We recommend that, at a minimum, the following cooperative efforts be undertaken:

5. Provide mutual diplomatic support to governments currently attempting to combat the drug traffic.
6. Following the recent suggestion of the French Finance Minister to attack "narco-money," cooperate in joint efforts to restrict the laundering of funds derived from the drug traffic.
7. Develop economic and financial models to better understand the flow of drugs and money deriving from the drug traffic.
8. Exchange information on the production, smuggling and distribution of narcotics, particularly, in Southeast and Central Asia and Latin America, in accordance with existing agreements.
9. Share technology and expertise on methods to interdict the illegal drug traffic.
10. Conduct further systematic studies of the phenomenon of "narco-terrorism."
11. Explore together the material and technical assistance requirements of countries that are on the front line in combatting drug production, in particular, Peru and Colombia.
12. Explore alternate ways to reduct the consumption of drug and the violence that accompanies the drug traffic.

Confronting Hostage Situations

Both Soviet and American citizens have been the victims of terrorist hostage takers abroad. Hostage situations are dangerous, not only because they place lives in peril, but because they can lead to international crisis. In several episodes in the recent past, the Soviet Union and the United States have cooperated to resolve hostage incidents and prevent their escalation into major international crises. In an effort to institutionalize that cooperation, we call upon our governments to:

13. Exchange information on Soviet and American citizens held against their will in the Middle East and Southeast Asia.
14. Convene a joint meeting to investigate means for securing the release of nationals of either country who are being held against their will.
15. Create the necessary machinery to facilitate continuing communication and cooperation in resolving future crises that may be caused by the seizure of hostages from either country.

Preventing Threats of Mass Destruction

The scientific and technical revolution may provide terrorists with the capability to use even more destructive means to carry out their criminal acts. To prevent terrorism, threatening or employing weapons of mass destruction, we recommend that our governments implement the following priority measures:

16. Enhance the effectiveness of the crisis centers created by the CBM Agreement to deal with a terrorist threat involving nuclear weapons or other means of mass destruction.
17. Exchange reports on the terrorist potential for the use of chemical, biological, radiological, or nuclear weapons.
18. Cooperate in technical and operational monitoring of events or developments that may indicate a danger of terrorist acquisition or use of any means of mass destruction.
19. Explore the possibility of sharing information on the technology of security for protecting civilian nuclear facilities.
20. Initiate joint diplomatic efforts aimed at preventing the development or sale of chemical, biological, and radiological weapons.

Controlling Terrorists' Movement and Financial Activities

The activities of terrorist organizations critically depend upon their freedom of movement across borders and their access to funds. Therefore, the group recommends that the governments of the United States and the Soviet Union:

21. Undertake cooperative efforts to restrict the movement and financial activities of terrorists.
22. Jointly raise the issue of countries that are "safe harbors" for terrorists in the current UNGA meeting and recommend that all countries adopt appropriate anti-terrorist legislation.

Continued Task Force Activities

Recognizing the achievements of the U.S.-Soviet Task Force to Prevent Terrorism in promoting a dialogue on cooperating against the threat of international terrorism, the Task Force will continue its efforts. It will:

23. Conduct a joint Soviet-U.S. simulation to explore the problems that might arise in responding to a terrorist-created crisis that involves both the United States and the Soviet Union.
24. Continue the unofficial Soviet and American dialogue on cooperating against terrorism as part of the broader international effort to combat the terrorist threat.
25. Enable American scholars to provide the Soviet Union with information on public opinion polls in the United States and other Western countries on the problem of terrorism and assist the Soviet Union in the conduct of such polling in the Soviet Union.
26. Initiate specific joint research projects on selected topics to be coordinated by the U.S.-Soviet Task Force.

Recommendations of the Legal Working Group:
Santa Monica, September 1989

Members:

ERIC GROVE

JOHN MURPHY

EUGENY LJAKHOV

VALENTIN ROMANOV

The governments of the United States and the Soviet Union should consider undertaking the following joint initiatives:

1. Narco-Terrorism

(a) Note with satisfaction the proposal introduced to the 44th session of the United Nations General Assembly by Trinidad-Tobago for the creation of an international judicial body to try persons accused of narcotics trafficking and associated acts of violence, especially in light of the Assembly's pending consideration of the item on international criminal jurisdiction.

(b) Promote cooperation between law enforcement authorities with respect to acts of violence associated with the trade in narcotics, through INTERPOL or other appropriate international institutions or by way of mutual consultations.

2. Technological Terrorism

(a) Initiate and sponsor a draft convention to define terrorism involving weapons of mass destruction, including in particular nuclear, radiological, chemical, and biological weapons, declare it a crime under international law, and obligate states parties to extradite or prosecute those who commit the crime.

(b) Make joint efforts within the United Nations, the International Atomic Energy Agency, and elsewhere to increase the number of states parties to the Convention on the Physical Protection of Nuclear Materials.

3. Hostages and Hijacking

(a) Negotiate a U.S.-Soviet bilateral agreement along the lines of the U.S.-Cuba Memorandum of Understanding on Hijacking of Aircraft and Vessels and Other Offenses, which incorporates the "extradite or prosecute" formula, but does so in a more meaningful way than do the multilateral anti-terrorism conventions.

(b) Support an initiative in the United Nations that would establish a committee that would oversee the implementation of the International Convention Against the Taking of Hostages.

(c) In light of the consensus on international terrorism recently arrived at in the Vienna Conference on Security and Cooperation in Europe, invite those states participating in the CSCE process which are not parties to the Bonn Declaration to consider acceding to it or applying its principles without acceding to the declaration.

4. Deliberate Targeting of Civilians

Initiate and sponsor a draft convention that would make the deliberate targeting of the civilian population an international crime.

Recommendations of the Middle East Working Group:
Santa Monica, September 1989

Members:

GEOFFREY KEMP

AUGUSTUS RICHARD NOR-
TON

ROBIN WRIGHT

ANDREY SHOUMIKHIN

The developing dialogue between the United States and the Soviet Union over the problem of terrorism is of obvious significance in the Middle East, the region which has, more than any other region, come to be viewed as a spawning ground for terrorism. The dialogue represents a serious attempt, by both sides, to grapple with a vexing and compelling problem. Moscow and Washington share an interest in preventing catalytic acts of violence which might not only derail the search for an Arab-Israeli peace but even provoke a new war. Each side is also intent on insuring the security of its citizens, whether they be diplomats or pilgrims. Because the U.S. and the USSR both stand to gain from this venture into bilateral cooperation, there are reasonable prospects for success.

U.S.-Soviet cooperation depends on a shared conception of what terrorism is and is not. The initial success of the dialogue stems from the explicit willingness of both sides to accept the principle that there are some forms of violence which are simply beyond the pale.

The problem with much of the discussion on terrorism is precisely that statesmen, editorial writers, and scholars too readily accept the shopworn cliché that one man's terrorist is another man's freedom fighter. If we use the term "terrorist" with the care and consistency which is warranted, one man's terrorist will simply be another man's terrorist. Terrorism is opprobrious by definition because of the innocence of its victims and the purposefully indiscriminate quality of its techniques.

A patent example would the anonymous car bomb exploded on a crowded shopping street. Parallel examples include the random shooting of civilian passengers in an airport departure lounge, the intentional mid-air bombing of a passenger plane, or the intentional slaughter of children or other non-combatants. In each of these examples it makes little difference where the incident occurs, what the nationality of the victims may be, or whether the perpetrator was a state or non-state actor. Each case is transparently clear. Naturally, it is possible to conceive of complicating factors which will cloud moral claims, but many acts are outright terrorism precisely because such complications do not exist.

Based on this common understanding of terrorism, we believe that practical cooperation between the U.S. and the Soviet Union to prevent, limit the damage, and punish such acts of terrorism are appropriate without compromising the national security interests of each nation in the region—and could be extended to other regions of the world. These measures could include the exchange of informational and analytical data that would contribute to both preventive and reactive actions against terrorists.

Terrorism thrives in the Middle East precisely because the region's conflicts nurture it. Both sides must, in cooperation with the regional antagonists, strive to help reach peaceful and negotiated settlements to the region's several conflicts, including the Arab-Israel conflict and that in Lebanon.

It would be very useful for government experts to jointly compare and assess their respective governments' arms transfer policies with a view toward preventing the transfer of weapons which might fall into the hands of terrorists.

In order to address the complex problem of hostages held captive in Lebanon, both sides should give consideration to the creation of an international humanitarian organization, with extensive participation from the states of the region, which would be chartered to pursue avenues of freedom for the hostages.

The ability of the international system to anticipate conflicts and crises which are likely to spawn acts of terrorism must be enhanced. In this regard, it is appropriate to explore the creation of an international warning center under the auspices of the United Nations. The U.S. and the USSR, in additional to other member states of the United Nations, could facilitate the operational effectiveness of such a center by the provision of technical and analytical assistance.

Proposal for the Establishment of a Working Group on Simulation:
Santa Monica, September 1989

Simulation: What is it?

A simulation is a role-playing exercise which structures reality in such a way as to enable the participants to model events and analyze them. Governments have long employed simulations as a tool of analysis. Such simulations have been played on an intergovernmental basis, including games concerning terrorism played by the U.S., U.K., FRG and Israel.

Objective

The objective of such a simulation would be to identify problems that would arise in a terrorist-caused crisis involving both the U.S. and the USSR.

Thrust

The simulation will consist of a realistic scenario that requires the U.S. and the USSR to explore a collaborative response. It will enable the exploration of the role of:

Areas

- Communication
- Government Organization
- Policy
- Domestic Political Considerations
- Diplomacy
- Legal, Domestic and International Requirements
- Dealing with the Public

Scenario

Candidate scenarios will be reviewed. Such scenarios will have the following components:

1. Demonstrate a compelling need for cooperation between the United States and the Soviet Union because the citizens and interests of both nations are directly and immediately involved.
2. Be politically rich and reflect complex international political and legal concerns.
3. Include third-party interests which affect the outcome of any possible actions chosen by the U.S. and the USSR.

A typical scenario might involve the hijacking of an airliner by a group in the employ of narco-traffickers. The passengers of that airline will include Soviet and American citizens. The airliner will be flown to a third country. The threat of the hijackers will be to kill Soviet and American citizens if the United States or Soviet Union does not comply with their demands.

Benefits: All Simulations

1. Sensitize the players to the decisions that are required in a time of real crisis.
2. Illustrate the benefits and risks of international cooperation.
3. Quickly display options for conflict resolution.
4. Show practical means and areas of cooperation.
5. Illustrate differing perceptions given the same data as input.
6. Suggest the limits of intelligence sharing.

Concept

The working group will construct two games, the first of which is private and informal for training and the second of which is more ambitious, formal, and complicated.

Action

We seek approval of the project in principle and recommend the establishment of a working group to produce the initial simulations. The working group, if approved, will consist of Soviet and American participants. The working group will set forth the financial requirements of the simulations.